909.82

TIME

2006
The Year in Review

By the Editors of TIME

The Year in Review

EDITOR	Kelly Knauer
DESIGNER	Ellen Fanning
PICTURE EDITOR	Patricia Cadley
WRITER/RESEARCH DIRECTOR	Matthew McCann Fenton
COPY EDITOR	Bruce Christopher Carr

TIME INC. HOME ENTERTAINMENT

PUBLISHER	Richard Fraiman
EXECUTIVE DIRECTOR, MARKETING SERVICES	Carol Pittard
DIRECTOR, RETAIL & SPECIAL SALES	Tom Mifsud
MARKETING DIRECTOR, BRANDED BUSINESSES	Swati Rao
DIRECTOR, NEW PRODUCT DEVELOPMENT	Peter Harper
FINANCIAL DIRECTOR	Steven Sandonato
BOOK PRODUCTION MANAGER	Jonathan Polsky
MARKETING MANAGER	Joy Butts
DESIGN & PREPRESS MANAGER	Anne-Michelle Gallero

SPECIAL THANKS TO

Bozena Bannett, Alexandra Bliss, Glenn Buonocore, Barbara Dudley Davis, Suzanne Janso, Joe Lertola, Robert Marasco, Brooke McGuire, Chavaughn Raines, Mary Sarro-Waite, Ilene Shreider, Adriana Tierno, Brooke Twyford

Copyright 2006 Time Inc. Home Entertainment
Published by TIME Books
Time Inc. • 1271 Avenue of the Americas • New York, NY 10020

We welcome your comments and suggestions about TIME Books. Please write to us at
TIME Books • Attention: Book Editors • PO Box 11016 • Des Moines, IA 50336-1016
ISSN: 1097-5721
ISBN 10: 1-933405-84-8
ISBN 13: 978-1-933405-84-1

If you would like to order any of our hardcover Collector's Edition books, please call us at 1-800-327-6388 (Monday through Friday, 7 a.m.–8 p.m., or Saturday, 7 a.m.–6 p.m., Central time).

PRINTED IN THE UNITED STATES OF AMERICA

COVER PHOTOGRAPHY CREDITS

FRONT COVER
Lebanon bombing: Kate Brooks—Polaris; Steve Irwin: Justin Sullivan—Getty Images; Condoleezza Rice: AP/Wide World; coal mine memorial: Ed Reinke—AP/Wide World; Mahmoud Ahmadinejad: AP/Wide World; Kim Jong Il: Xinhua—AP/Wide World; Andre Agassi: Bob Martin—SPORTS ILLUSTRATED

BACK COVER
Tiger Woods: Carl De Souza—AFP—Getty Images; Shaun White: Mike Powell—Getty Images; Ann Richards: Pam Francis—Getty Images; Amish funeral procession: Thomas Kelly IV—Polaris

TIME

—— 2006 ——
The Year in Review

YEARNING TO BREATHE FREE: On April 10, 2006, some 100,000 demonstrators rallied in the nation's capital to protest proposed legislation that would make many undocumented immigrants felons

By the Editors of TIME

Contents

2006: The Year in Review

IMAGES vi
A retrospective of the year's most memorable photographs

Nation
FACES: DONALD RUMSFELD 18
FACES: MARK FOLEY 19
FACES: JOHN McCAIN 20
FACES: HILLARY CLINTON 21
VOICE OF THE PEOPLE 22
Americans visit the polls in a turning-point midterm election
MAN ON THE MARGINS 26
Isolated on Iraq and losing touch with the G.O.P. faithful,
George W. Bush becomes Washington's Lone Ranger
CAPITOL OFFENSES 28
Voters recoil as corruption and come-ons rock Congress
IRAQ: STILL SEARCHING FOR THE WAY FORWARD 30
Three years ... and counting: as Iraq descends to the brink of
civil war, 144,000 U.S. troops fight to keep the nation stable
NATION NOTES 36

World
FACES: MAHMOUD AHMADINEJAD 40
FACES: HUGO CHAVEZ 41
FACES: HASSAN NASRALLAH 42
FACES: NOURI AL-MALIKI 43
BOMBS OVER LEBANON 44
In a long-anticipated showdown, Israel launches a mini-war
against Hizballah militants in its neighbor to the north
NUCLEAR TREMORS IN ASIA 48
North Korea rocks the world by testing a nuclear bomb
IRAN DREAMS OF GRANDEUR 50
President Mahmoud Ahmadinejad stirs up his nation's
Islamists while refusing to halt research into nuclear power
TERRORISTS HIT BOMBAY 52
India blames Muslim militants for a July 11 attack that sets off
bombs on commuter railways, killing more than 180 people
WORLD NOTES 54

Person of the Year
THE MOST INFLUENTIAL INDIVIDUAL OF 2006: YOU! . . . 56
The Internet's latest incarnation brings power to the people

Society
FACES: WARREN BUFFETT 72
FACES: KENNETH LAY 73
FACES: KATIE COURIC 74
FACES: KATHARINE J. SCHORI 75
IMMIGRATION: AMERICA'S NEW DIVIDING LINE 76
As demonstrators march in U.S. streets, Congress aims to
pass comprehensive reforms but cannot reach consensus
TABLOID TEMPESTS 80
Brangelina, TomKat and Mel Gibson: the year in stargazing
SOCIETY NOTEBOOK 82

Sport
FACES: ROGER FEDERER 86
FACES: ALBERT PUJOLS 87
FACES: DWYANE WADE 88

FACES: BEN ROETHLISBERGER 89
BRAVISSIMO, TORINO! 90
The Winter Olympics offer X-game thrills and showboat spills
PAR FOR THE COURSE 94
In golf's year, Phil Mickelson chokes, Tiger Woods keeps on
roaring and the Europeans refuse to part with the Ryder Cup
COLOR US RED, WHITE AND VERY, VERY BLUE 96
Soccer's World Cup is sport's most colorful quadrennial event,
even if you're cheering for the Stars and Stripes
HEROES OR VILLAINS? 98
Barry Bonds, Floyd Landis and the rest: in modern sport you
can't tell the good guys from the bad guys without a drug test
SPORT NOTES 100

Science
FACES: AL GORE 104
FACES: ZAHI HAWASS 105
THE YEAR'S HOTTEST STORY 106
Concerns over global warming finally enter the mainstream
EARTH TO PLUTO: GET LOST 110
The loneliest planet gets even lonelier
STEM CELLS: THE PROMISES AND THE PROTESTS 112
Embryonic-stem-cell research launches hopes—and hype
SCIENCE NOTES 116

The Arts
FACES: JOHNNY DEPP 120
FACES: MERYL STREEP 121
FACES: HEATH LEDGER 122
FACES: PETER GELB 123
THINKING OUT OF THE BOX 124
The year in architecture: new forms revive old cities
RUN FOR YOUR LIVES! THE BLOCKBUSTERS ARE HERE . 126
Hollywood's formula for the multiplex each summer:
sequels, prequels and things that blow up real good
OLD WINE, NEW BOTTLES 128
Bob Dylan and the Dixie Chicks release strong new albums,
while a chipper chef and a bogus bigfoot brighten up the tube
THE BYGONE BLUES 130
Broadway thrives on a steady diet of revivals, recycled
Disney films, visiting movie stars and jukebox musicals
ARTS NOTES 132

Milestones
STEVE IRWIN 134
SLOBODAN MILOSEVIC 136
CORETTA SCOTT KING 137
ANN RICHARDS 138
BETTY FRIEDAN 139
ED BRADLEY 140
MILTON FRIEDMAN 141
JOHN KENNETH GALBRAITH 142
SUSAN BUTCHER 143
WILLIAM STYRON 144
ROBERT ALTMAN 145
GORDON PARKS 146
WENDY WASSERSTEIN 147
BRIEF LIVES 148

SEMPER FI: A member of a U.S. Marine honor guard holds the flag during burial services for Sergeant Justin Walsh of Cuyahoga Falls, Ohio, at Arlington National Cemetery in Virginia on Oct. 24, 2006. Walsh was fatally wounded while attempting to defuse a bomb in Iraq. With 105 deaths, October was the deadliest month of 2006 for U.S. soldiers serving in the unsettled land

Philadelphia, June 28

Sinking Feeling

In recent years Americans have turned their eyes to the South to witness a string of major weather disasters, from the four mighty hurricanes that struck Florida and the Gulf Coast in 2004 to the unforgettable calamities caused by Hurricane Katrina in 2005. But in 2006 Mother Nature visited her wrath upon the states of the mid-Atlantic region, as several early-summer floods surged across a broad swath of land from Massachusetts and upstate New York to Virginia and North Carolina, killing 20 people, forcing hundreds of thousands of people from their homes and leaving an estimated $1 billion in damages in their wake.

At left, the waters of the Schuylkill River in Philadelphia overrun the lower floors of the historic, illuminated Victorian buildings along Boathouse Row, which occupy an elevated position along the riverside. The landmark buildings are home of the Schuylkill Navy, a foundation of America's rowing community since 1858. The National Weather Service termed the 2006 events a 200-year flood; let's hope so.

**JOHN COSTELLO—
PHILADELPHIA INQUIRER—WPN**

Last Stand

Over the course of the past few years, Israeli Prime Minister Ariel Sharon, long known as a hawk regarding Israel's occupation of the Palestinian territories of Gaza and the West Bank, surprised the world by changing his policy. Under Sharon's unilateral plan, Israel began withdrawing from settlements established in Gaza and building security barriers to keep terrrorists from venturing into Israel. The withdrawal from Israeli settlements in Gaza was completed with surprisingly little fuss in August 2005. But in February 2006, after Israel's Supreme Court ruled that nine homes built near the town of Ramallah in the West Bank had been erected without government permission and should thus be demolished, some settlers resisted. At right, a phalanx of Israeli security officers do battle with an outnumbered yet defiant female settler.

By year's end, events had moved far beyond this scene. Sharon was felled by a major stroke in January and never recovered. His successor, Ehud Olmert, launched a blitz on Hizballah militia forces in Lebanon in July after two Israeli soldiers were taken hostage. Israel's new, tougher policies made the passions that animated the year's first months seem like scenes from a distant past.

ODED BALILTY—AP/WIDE WORLD

Ramallah, West Bank, Feb. 1

Hope, Ark., June 2

Hopeless

As Americans observed the first anniversary of Hurricane Katrina's 2005 assault on New Orleans and the Gulf Coast, passions were still running high over the response of civic, state and federal leaders to the greatest natural disaster to strike the U.S. in decades. Those looking for symbols of the inept federal reaction to Katrina pointed to pictures like this one, which shows some 10,770 mobile homes purchased by the Federal Emergency Management Agency (FEMA) to house homeless New Orleanians, but never put to use. As of June, 2006, the trailers were still sitting, untenanted, at the Hope Municipal Airport in Hope, Ark.

Fortunately, the summer portion of the 2006 hurricane season came and went without a major tropical storm hitting the U.S. But those who lived through Katrina are still dealing with its legacy: TIME's Cathy Booth Thomas reported that among Katrina survivors, depression is common, the suicide rate has nearly tripled, domestic abuse is rising, and self-medicating with liquor is a favored method of avoiding haunting memories.

ROBERT KING—POLARIS

Bombs Away, Again

Lebanese men watch in dismay as Israeli jets bomb the Rafik Hariri Airport in Beirut. The bombings were part of an offensive launched by Israel against Lebanon's Hizballah Party, which has been consolidating its potent military presence in the southern portion of the nation in the six years since Israel withdrew in 2000 from a security zone it had held there since 1982. Israeli Prime Minister Ehud Olmert made the decision to strike Hizballah after two Israeli soldiers were kidnapped on July 12, sending some 1,000 air sorties over Lebanon in 24 hours. In the conflict that followed, Israeli tanks and troops rolled into Lebanon and Hizballah sent rockets raining down on cities in northern Israel, forcing an estimated 1 million Israelis from their homes.

The mini-war was brought to a conclusion on Aug. 14 by a cease-fire brokered by the United Nations, but not before Lebanon and its capital, Beirut—which had spent the past decade re-building from the civil war that ravaged the country from 1975 until 1990—suffered damages estimated to reach as high as $3.5 billion. The crisis proved that Hizballah and its sponsors in Iran and Syria hold more power in many parts of Lebanon than the weak official government.

KATE BROOKS—POLARIS

Beirut, Lebanon, July 16

Wake-up Call

Lying along the famed Ring of Fire—where the slow-motion collision of giant tectonic plates creates a "hot zone" for volcanoes and earthquakes—the islands of the southeast Indian Ocean are geologically prone to natural disasters. The vast region seems to have been particularly unsettled in recent years; the tsunami that killed more than 225,000 people on Dec. 26, 2004, was only the most memorable of a spate of geological calamities that has afflicted the area.

Two mighty earthquakes rocked Indonesia's island of Java in 2006. The first hit just before 6 a.m., local time, on May 27, 15 miles southwest of the city of Yogyakarta, on Java's south shore. The quake's magnitude was measured at 6.3—enough to leave more than 6,000 people dead, some 36,000 injured and 1.5 million homeless in the densely populated region.

At right, a boy eats breakfast amid the ruins of his home in the hard-hit city of Bantul, south of Yogyakarta, two days after the disaster. Fortunately, no tsunami followed the event—but some seven weeks later, another big earthquake did. A 7.7-magnitude monster rocked the seas south of Java, spawning a tsunami that killed more than 650 people.

DAVID LONGSTREATH—
AP/WIDE WORLD

Bantul, Indonesia, May 29

Berlin, July 9

The Joy of Victory, the Agony of the Head-Butt

Take that! When France's superstar midfielder Zinédine Zidane smashed his bald noggin into the chest of Italy's Marco Materazzi in the waning minutes of overtime in soccer's World Cup final match, it was the cheap shot heard round the world. More than 1 billion TV viewers saw the outrageous act of poor sportsmanship live—and watched it again and again in instant replay. Given that the World Cup final is the world's most-watched sporting event, Zidane's act provided weeks of fodder for pundits, editorial cartoonists and late-night comics. The gnarly "Zizou," as his fans call him, had become a hero to the French after his sterling play in the 1998 tournament helped bring the trophy to Paris, while his background as the son of Algerian immigrants brought a welcome sense of unity to a nation recently riven over the problems posed by its increasing cultural differences.

Zidane had his defenders, including TIME's Bill Saporito, who pointed out that Materazzi (called *l'animale* by Italian fans) is well known to be a thug on the field. Saporito called for the game's governing body, the Federation Internationale de Football Association (FIFA), to halt the fouls and trash talking, some of it racist, that he believes disfigure the current game. Indeed, Zidane claimed after the incident that Materazzi had provoked him by insulting his family, but would say no more. Weeks later, Materazzi offered his side of the story: he claimed that he had grabbed Zidane's shirt and the French star told him, "If you want, I'll give you the jersey later" (an exchange of jerseys is a postgame ritual for players). Materazzi's reply: "I'd prefer your sister." Zizou's response: BAM! Confounding the moral confusion over the headstrong deed, FIFA later awarded to the retiring Zidane the golden ball traditionally given to the tournament's best player .

Phil's Rough Patch

Tiger Woods commands the respect of all golf fans, but the man the galleries really love is the left-handed golfer with the big wide grin, Phil Mickelson. Fans embrace "Lefty" because he wears his heart on his sleeve—and because he sometimes seems to be just another duffer, hitting the stray clunker that ruins a great round. Mickelson finally beat the charge that he couldn't win major tournaments by taking the 2004 Masters and 2005 PGA championships; he then led off 2006 by donning the green jacket of the Masters winner a second time. So fans fervently hoped he had at last whipped his demons.

At the year's second major, the U.S. Open at Winged Foot in Westchester, N.Y., Mickelson was leading Briton Geoff Ogilvy by a stroke as he stood on the 18th tee in the final round; even a bogey would have won the Open. Alas! Mickelson hooked his drive far left, deep into the rough, and rather than safely pitching his second shot onto the fairway, he tried to force the ball through the trees to the green. BONK! The ball hit a tree and rebounded; a wasted shot. After his next shot plunked into a greenside bunker, Lefty carded a double bogey and lost the coveted trophy. The man's rueful, uncontested comment: "I am such an idiot."

Winged Foot Golf Club, Mamaroneck, N.Y., June 18

Philippi, W.Va., Jan. 6

Tears in Coal-Mine Country

Tragedy struck 13 times in Sago, W.Va., on Jan. 2, 2006. The first 12 tragedies were harsh enough: after an explosion in the Sago Coal Mine, 13 miners were trapped deep beneath the earth. As wives, children, neighbors and friends gathered at the Sago Baptist Church to wait for news from a rescue team struggling to find them, the rescuers reached the cavern where the miners had been trapped and found that only one of the 13 men was alive.

Now came the final, more punishing tragedy; a rumor based on an overheard cell-phone call reached the church that all 13 men had been found alive, setting off a joyous celebration and prayers of thanks. Three hours later, Ben Hatfield, president of the mine's owner, the International Coal Group, told the crowd that in fact only Randal McCloy had survived. At left, Bill Stemple remembers four men from nearby Barbour County who died in the explosion. The mine's owners had received 208 citations of safety violations from a federal watchdog agency in the year before the tragedy occurred.

ED REINKE—AP/WIDE WORLD

Nation

"I don't think there's anybody here who wants to do anything but forgive ... and ... to reach out to

Paradise Lost

Pennsylvania's Amish people are widely respected for pursuing horse-and-buggy lives in a motorized age. So Americans' hearts fell on Oct. 2, as a shocking headline hit the Internet: GUNMAN HOLDS HOSTAGES IN AMISH SCHOOL. The news got worse: before taking his own life at the one-room school in West Nickel Mines, Pa., Charles C. Roberts IV, 32, killed five schoolgirls and wounded five others. Survivor Barbie Fisher, 9, who escaped, reported that her sister Marian, at 13 the oldest hostage, asked to be shot first in the hope that Roberts would let the younger girls go. The Fisher family invited Roberts' widow to the funeral, in hopes of consoling her.

the family of the man who committed these acts." —Jack Meyer, member of the local Amish community

Donald Rumsfeld

"Put your head down, do the best job possible, let the flak pass and work toward [your] goals." —Rumsfeld

A Secretary on the Defensive

FOR THE MOST CONTROVERSIAL SECRETARY OF DEFENSE IN recent memory, 2006 will be recalled as a year in which he was plagued by rebellious generals and rogue states. The generals were senior U.S. military officers who chafed at Donald Rumsfeld's handling of the Iraq war and felt free to speak their minds from the safety of retirement. The "states," in this case, were two books: *State of War,* which arrived in stores (and the headlines) in January, and *State of Denial,* published in October. The first, by New York *Times* reporter James Risen, revealed a massive, warrantless domestic spying program conducted by the Defense Department's National Security Agency. The second, by Washington *Post* veteran reporter Bob Woodward, charted the chaotic management of the Iraqi occupation on Rumsfeld's watch. Both portrayed President George W. Bush as in thrall to his underling, unwilling to cut his losses by firing the architect of what is now widely regarded as a fiasco. Risen's book told of Bush's angrily hanging up the telephone on his father when the former President lectured him about "allowing ... Rumsfeld and a cadre of neoconservative ideologues to exert broad influence over foreign policy." Woodward claimed that both First Lady Laura Bush and White House chief of staff Andrew Card privately lobbied the President to dump Rumsfeld in 2004 and '05.

Yet the book buzz, which Rumsfeld called carping, was a sideshow compared with the criticism leveled at him by a group of former high-ranking officers. Army General John Batiste, who commanded the 1st Infantry Division in Iraq, told TIME in April that, "every time I looked at him, I was thinking about ... that s___ war plan, I was thinking about Abu Ghraib, and I was thinking about the challenges I had every day trying to rebuild the Iraqi military that he disbanded." The same month, retired General Greg Newbold wrote in TIME, "We need fresh ideas and fresh faces. That means, as a first step, replacing Rumsfeld ..." More than a dozen former generals joined this choir, aided by members of Congress. But as Bush showed what TIME political columnist Joe Klein termed "suicidal loyalty" to the Pentagon chief, Rumsfeld dismissed their dissent with a blithe "this too shall pass." In the end, though, it was "Rummy" who passed; the President announced his resignation on Nov. 8, one day after the Republicans' huge loss in the midterm elections. ∎

Mark Foley

"The instant messages … are vile and repulsive to me and to my colleagues." —House Speaker Dennis Hastert

Downfall of a Predatory Politician

DO I MAKE YOU A LITTLE HORNY?" CONGRESSMAN MARK Foley, 52, wrote to the teenage boy serving as a page in the U.S. House of Representatives in an e-mail message. In another, he asked, "You in your boxers, too? … well, strip down and get relaxed." When those private words hit the public airwaves, they put a quick end to the career of a self-styled defender of children against sexual predators. Americans of all political stripes were shocked by the blatant hypocrisy of the closeted gay politician, who had run under the banner of a party that has thrived by publicizing its opposition to civil rights for homosexuals.

Before his fall, the suave Foley was a fast-rising six-term moderate Republican from Florida who chaired the House Missing and Exploited Children's Caucus and was considered a likely future Senate candidate. When ABC News revealed on Sept. 28 that he had for several years been badgering teenage boys working on Capitol Hill with online come-ons, he became the living embodiment of the timeworn political adage that deems congressional seats so safe

for incumbents that the only way to lose one is "to get caught with a dead girl or a live boy." The day after the e-mails were revealed, Foley resigned from the House, declared he was an alcoholic who had been sexually abused in his youth and checked himself into a rehabilitation program.

Foley did not appear to have broken any laws. Lewd computer messages between adults and minors are not a violation of any federal statute, as long as they don't lead to sexual contact, and, as of late October 2006, no one had thus far alleged that Foley's misconduct was anything other than virtual. (In another irony, Foley sponsored legislation in the summer of 2005 to shield children from adult exploitation over the Internet, but it was never enacted.)

In a statement released on the day he resigned his seat, a repentant Foley apologized for "letting down my family and the people of Florida." He might have added to that list the millions of conservative voters around the nation who had believed in his party's claim of holding the moral high ground, only to be misled by one they called their own. ∎

John McCain

"In a field of uninspiring alternatives, [voters] will prefer electable McCain to the looming Hillary Clinton." —Ralph Nader

A Political Maverick Takes Aim at the Mainstream

ACCUSING THE BUSH ADMINISTRATION OF ENCOURAGING the belief that the U.S. intervention in Iraq would be "some kind of day at the beach," Senator John McCain said in August, "It grieves me so much that we had not told the American people how tough and difficult this task would be." Yet in almost the same breath, McCain added that he still strongly supported the war. If that position seems a tad nuanced, welcome to the world of McCain: he is a self-described conservative who has alienated the G.O.P.'s right wing with heresies like opposition to the Bush tax cuts and support for campaign spending limits; he is also a foreign policy hawk who championed anti-torture legislation widely seen as a rebuke to the President. McCain, in short, is vastly more complicated, and far harder to hang a label on, than the headlines that he creates.

But if his defining characteristics—independence and single-mindedness—don't always play well with political insiders (McCain lost the 2000 G.O.P. nomination by frightening both his party's establishment leaders and its religious base), they have earned him enormous moral authority. By now, the details of the 5½ years he survived in a North Vietnamese POW camp are well known: McCain, 70, still suffers from the tortures he endured there.

McCain's reputation for gravitas rests on a broad foundation. He has chosen to devote much of his two-decade Senate career to problems that are both entrenched and unexciting. In the process, he has challenged the rules in Washington and the cynicism of voters at home. He also has a knack for political troublemaking: in 2005 he took the backwater committee he chaired, Indian Affairs, and used it to launch an investigation of lobbyist Jack Abramoff, whose fall unleashed a political cataclysm for Republicans. McCain may be just the man to pick up the pieces. The best funded and perhaps most admired of all serious contenders for the Republican presidential nod in 2008, he is also widely regarded as the candidate most likely to beat the Democrat's presumptive (but, like McCain, undeclared) front runner: Senator Hillary Clinton. ■

Hillary Clinton

"He [Bill Clinton] thinks that she should run, and he's going to do everything possible to help her." —Friend Bernard Rapoport

Campaigning for the Senate—and Maybe Something More?

AS SHE CAMPAIGNED FOR RE-ELECTION TO THE SENATE in 2006, New York's Hillary Rodham Clinton appeared to be laying all the necessary groundwork for a possible run for the White House in 2008. In part to deflect the attacks of Hillary haters around the country, she formed alliances with Republicans who once spat out her name like a curse. And she quietly built a nationwide fund-raising network capable of bringing in at least $40 million for her 2006 race and probably far more in the crucial 18 months that will follow. Clinton has won glowing reviews from all sides for her hard work in the Senate, and in 2005 she emerged as the party's most sought-after speaker. Her single stumble in 2006 was a strained metaphor in which she compared the G.O.P.-controlled House of Representatives to a Southern plantation.

Polls show that Clinton remains the candidate both Democrats and left-leaning independents prefer to win the party's nod in 2008. As for the G.O.P., her Republican Senate colleague Lindsey Graham wrote for TIME in May, "The mere thought of a Hillary Clinton presidential bid is shaping Republican primary politics for 2008." Yet many observers in both parties believe she cannot win in 2008, because she is simply too divisive a figure. Her strategists counter that all she would have to do in November 2008 is win every state John Kerry did in 2004, plus one more.

While the early line is that Hillary would be unstoppable in a Democratic primary but unelectable in a general election, an August TIME poll showed that in hypothetical matchups with the early G.O.P. favorite, John McCain, Clinton was the only big-name Democrat to make a real race of it, with McCain edging her by just 2 points among registered voters. (The same poll showed McCain would trounce Kerry by 10 points and Gore by 9.)

There's another man Clinton has to watch out for—her husband. No one who knows either Clinton has any idea how to bring a man renowned for his voracious need for information into anything approaching the marginal role of political spouse. Yet Bill Clinton is also widely regarded as the most astute political thinker of his generation. Let the G.O.P. see red: the Clintons' dreams are white. ■

A Wake-up Call for

The Democrats take control of both houses of Congress, as voters send a strong message for change to President George W. Bush and his party

NEARLY FOUR YEARS OF ONE-PARTY RULE CAME TO AN end on Tuesday, Nov. 7, as Americans touched their screens, filled out their ballots—and voted for historic change in Washington and state capitals around the country. The final results of the election—including the winner of a key Senate race, which decided the control of the upper house of Congress—were not known until two days after voters went to the polls. But when the dust cleared, the Democrats found themselves in control of both houses of Congress and in possession of a majority of the nation's governorships.

As Americans woke up on Nov. 8, there were clear signs of a possible Democratic sweep. The party's candidates had captured four of the six Republican seats they needed to control the Senate and held tiny but serviceable margins in Virginia and Montana, the two states where the counting continued. By mid-afternoon they had picked up one of those seats, in Montana. In Virginia, Democrat Jim Webb was holding a lead of slightly more than 7,000 votes over Republican George Allen. Yet even before the outcome in Virginia was known, it was already clear that voters around the nation had sent a resounding message of disapproval to the Republican Party. The final results amounted to the single biggest setback of George W. Bush's presidency: they will deprive him of a governing majority in Washington and raise new doubts about his effectiveness and agenda during his final two years in office.

The election reflected all the trials—both metaphorical

VICTORY! Nancy Pelosi, who is in line to be the next Speaker of the House, celebrates the Democrats' big night with the heads of the party's congressional campaign committees, Representative Rahm Emanuel of Illinois, left, and Senator Chuck Schumer of New York

the G.O.P.

DeLay; the convictions of lobbyist Jack Abramoff, California Representative Randy (Duke) Cunningham and Ohio Representative Bob Ney; and the sex scandal surrounding Florida Congressman Mark Foley. All were Republicans.

The anti-G.O.P. tide became evident early in the evening of Nov. 7, as Democrats took away the Governors' seats in Massachusetts, Ohio and New York (where potential 2008 Democratic presidential contender Hillary Clinton won re-election to the Senate by a resounding margin). Democrats will control at least 28 Governor's mansions in 2007.

The movement to the Democrats extended from the state to the national level: by Wednesday afternoon, the Democrats had achieved a 29-seat gain in the House of Representatives, with 10 contests undecided. The range of the victory was as telling as its size: the Democrats picked up seats in traditionally G.O.P. districts in Indiana, Kentucky, Connecticut, Florida, Pennsylvania and Ohio.

In the Senate, Democrats seized three of the six seats they needed to take control of the chamber by midway through Tuesday evening, as voters rejected Republican incumbents in Rhode Island, Ohio and Pennsylvania. Early Wednesday morning, Missouri state auditor Claire McCaskill claimed victory over incumbent Republican Senator Jim Talent; hours later, state senator Jon Tester was declared the victor over incumbent Republican Conrad Burns in Montana.

Now all eyes were trained on Virginia, where many expected that the race between Democratic challenger Webb and incumbent Republican Allen might not be resolved until late in November. But Allen conceded victory to Webb on the afternoon of Nov. 9, ensuring that the Democrats would control both houses of Congress for the first time in 12 years.

The historic turnabout brought a definitive end to the Republican Revolution that began in 1994 with an equally significant congressional victory as a President from the oppo-

and literal—that had dogged the Bush Administration and the G.O.P.-led Congress in the past two years. Perhaps above all, the swing to the Democrats amounted to a strong vote of no confidence on the war in Iraq, which has claimed more than 2,800 American lives and left more than 20,000 troops injured almost four years after its beginning. The President signaled almost immediately that he had received that message, declaring in a White House press conference on Wednesday afternoon that he would accept the resignation of Defense Secretary Donald Rumsfeld, chief architect of U.S. strategy in the unpopular war *(see following story)*.

The results also suggested that Americans were unhappy with the federal response to Hurricane Katrina and the explosion of the deficit on the Republican watch. Another key factor on voters' minds was the stench of corruption that had fouled the House of Representatives, which peaked with the indictment and resignation of House majority leader Tom

JEFF ROBERSON—AP/WIDE WORLD

STEPPING DOWN: House Speaker Dennis Hastert, 64, prepares to speak with supporters at a campaign rally in Illinois. On Nov. 8 he said he would not seek re-election to the Republican leadership when the new Congress takes office in January 2007. The low-key Hastert was badly damaged by questions about how much he had known about the sex scandal surrounding Florida's Mark Foley

THE DAY AFTER: President Bush speaks at a White House press conference on Nov. 8, at which he announced he would accept the resignation of his embattled Defense Secretary, Donald Rumsfeld

site party held the White House. That revolution lost its way. Newt Gingrich's original rebels swept into Washington on the promise that they would change Capitol Hill, and for a time, they did. Vowing to finish what Ronald Reagan had started, they stood firm on the three principles that defined his brand of conservatism: fiscal responsibility, national security and moral values. Reagan, who suffered a few scandals in his day, didn't always follow his own rules. But his doctrine offered a good set of talking points for winning elections in an evenly divided country, and the takeover was completed with the Inauguration of George W. Bush as President.

But by the time it had controlled both houses of Congress and the White House for most of Bush's six years in office, the party had become unmoored from its Grand Old ideals. To win votes back home, Republican lawmakers who branded the Democrats as big spenders had been handing out tax-payer money like sailors on leave, producing the biggest

budget deficits in U.S. history. The exquisitely divisive polit-ical machinery the G.O.P. used to drive repeated triumphs in elections had begun to betray its own calls for national uni-ty. The party's approach to national security had taken the country into a war that most Americans now believe was a mistake and that the government's own intelligence experts say has shaped "a new generation of terrorist leaders and op-eratives." And the party that came to Washington to clean up a corrupt institution ran into scandals of its own.

After the Republicans took power, the system began to change them, rather than the other way around. Among the first promises they broke was their goal of setting term lim-its. And their longtime frustrations in the minority didn't make them open to reaching across the aisle to work with De-mocrats. Compromise, that most central of congressional checks and balances, was largely replaced by a kind of cal-culated cussedness that left the G.O.P. isolated and exposed in times of crisis. Such a crisis arrived late in September, only weeks before the election. The sex scandal involving the sug-gestive e-mail messages sent by Florida Representative Foley to teenage male House pages muddied one of the party's few remaining patches of moral high ground: its defense of fam-ily values and personal accountability.

Democrats, who had been smarting since their narrow losses of the White House in 2000 and '04, were wearing big grins after the election, and rightly so. But it seemed clear that the historic reversal at the nation's polls was driven more by voters' disgust with the Republicans than their admiration for the Democrats. The outcome presented a clear challenge to the newly empowered party: Democrats would have to go beyond merely criticizing the President and prove to voters they had a constructive agenda of their own. Americans had voted for change, and against the status quo; they had voted for progress, not more polarization. But whether politicians on both sides of the aisle who had long wielded partisanship for political advantage could learn to forsake cussedness and embrace civility remained to be seen. ∎

Lady of the House

"The campaign is over," a grinning Nancy Pelosi shouted triumphantly on the evening of Nov. 7 to hundreds of roaring supporters. "Democrats are ready to lead!" And no one was more ready than the House minority leader of four years, who is poised to take over as America's first female Speaker of the House in the 110th Congress.

The honor capped a rapid rise for a politician who didn't run for office until she was 47. Pelosi grew up in a prominent political family in Baltimore, Md., where her father was the mayor for almost her entire childhood. After college, Pelosi and husband Paul moved to New York City and then to San Francisco, where she became a leading Democratic fund raiser, then chairwoman of the state party. But she waited until the youngest of her five children was a high school senior before she ran for Congress in 1987.

Like Tom DeLay, the ousted Republican majority leader with whom she often jousted, Pelosi embraces hard-knuckle partisanship. She once described her approach as, "If people are ripping your face off, you have to rip their face off." When asked early in 2006 about the major benefits of a Democratic takeover of Congress, she blurted out, "Subpoena power."

Yet preliminary indications are that Pelosi intends to focus on consensus issues that will unite most Democrats and maybe draw some Republican crossover votes. Among them: raising the minimum wage, lowering interest rates on student loans, enacting recommendations from the 9/11 commission that the Bush Administration ignored, allowing the Federal Government to negotiate for better prices for prescription drugs and facilitating stem-cell research. As for harnessing wayward Democrats to a larger agenda, Pelosi told TIME in August, "They listen to no one … they don't listen to each other." Note to the new majority: Listen up!

Senate Scorecard

After cliff-hanger wins in Montana and Virginia, Democrats hold 49 seats; two independent Senators will caucus with them, giving them 51 votes

The Winners

Joe Lieberman, Conn.

The former vice-presidential candidate rallied from a loss in the Democratic primary. Running as an independent, he went on to beat wealthy executive Ned Lamont.

Claire McCaskill, Mo.

The Democrat state auditor defeated incumbent Jim Talent in a squeaker the White House had hoped to win; Bush campaigned with Talent as the election neared.

Bob Corker, Tenn.

The Republican former mayor of Chattanooga found himself locked in a seesaw duel with Democrat Harold Ford but pulled out a victory by 3 percentage points.

Robert Menendez, N.J.

The Democrat was appointed to fill the seat vacated by Jon Corzine in January 2006. He defeated Thomas Kean Jr., son of the popular former Governor, 53% to 45%.

The Losers

Rick Santorum, Pa.

The strongly conservative Republican, beloved by the right and hated by the left, was handily beaten by Bob Casey Jr., son of the state's former Governor.

Lincoln Chafee, R.I.

The moderate Republican was respected by members of both parties, yet he was swept aside in the strong Democratic tide, losing to Sheldon Whitehouse.

Harold Ford Jr., Tenn.

One of the Democrats' most promising candidates, House member Ford, who is black, weathered a campaign marred by smear tactics, losing to Bob Corker.

Mike DeWine, Ohio

Polls showed the Republican incumbent was trailing challenger Sherrod Brown all along, and his final loss reflected those numbers: Brown 56%, DeWine, 44%.

Two Close Calls

Conrad Burns, Mont.

The Republican incumbent from Montana was locked in a very tight race with challenger Jon Tester; he ended up losing by a whisker in the final tallies.

Jon Tester, Mont.

The Democrat and president of the Montana state senate declared victory over Burns on Nov. 8, giving Democrats (and the two independents) 50 seats in the U.S. Senate.

George Allen, Va.

The Republican incumbent, son of a famed football coach, stumbled more than once during the campaign and ended up narrowly losing to opponent Jim Webb.

Jim Webb, Va.

The ex-Marine, who served as Ronald Reagan's Secretary of Defense, claimed victory on the morning of Nov. 9; after a few hours, Allen conceded defeat.

Moving to the Margin

A diminished President replaces his Defense Secretary, promises fresh perspectives on problems and calls on figures from the past for counsel

ON WEDNESDAY MORNING, NOV. 8, PRESIDENT GEORGE W. Bush picked up the phone in the White House and made two difficult calls. The first was to outgoing House Speaker Dennis Hastert of Illinois. According to a deputy press secretary, the President thanked the Speaker for his leadership and told him, "While we came up short, we're committed to working with Democrats to get things done for the country." The second call was tougher: Bush spoke with incoming Democratic Speaker Nancy Pelosi of California, and the two agreed they would work together for the good of the nation in the final two years of Bush's presidency.

Bush's courtesy call to Pelosi was a ritual of U.S. political life; beyond the formalities, TIME White House correspondent Mike Allen reported, Bush planned to respond to the Republican wipeout in the midterm elections with a combination of conciliation and firmness. In that approach, Allen suggested, Bush would face a difficult challenge in his quest to pacify an empowered and emboldened opposition.

At an East Room press conference Wednesday afternoon, Bush was firm indeed, as he cast loose Defense Secretary Donald Rumsfeld, who resigned his position after nearly six years at the helm of the Pentagon. Bush named Robert Gates, the former head of the CIA, as Rumsfeld's replacement. The President was also conciliatory, taking some of the blame for the G.O.P.'s stinging defeat, saying, "As the head of the Republican Party, I share a large part of the responsibility. I told my party's leaders that it is now our duty to put the elections behind us and work together with the Democrats and independents on the great issues facing this country."

Bush went on to address the voters' concerns directly: "The message yesterday was clear. The American people want their leaders in Washington to set aside partisan differences, conduct ourselves in an ethical manner and work together to address the challenges facing our nation."

What would that mean for the future? "The same group of problems are there," White House press secretary Tony Snow told TIME. "You just will have some different people in the leadership. We have an opportunity to have an activist last two years of this presidency, which will be good for the country." Snow challenged Democrats, saying they would now have to "decide whether they're going to be part of the solution or are going to try to shut down the government for two years and point fingers at the President."

Snow also pointed to the halcyon days when Bush was Texas Governor and running for President back in 2000, when supporters applauded his jocular and productive relations with Democrats in the state legislature as signs that he could be what the campaign called "a uniter, not a divider."

"The accurate model for this White House will be the Texas experience, where he worked effectively with Democrats, to their mutual benefit," Snow said. But officials in both parties say that will be awfully hard to replicate in the bitterly partisan atmosphere of 2006, fostered in part by the Bush team. The President met with Pelosi at the White House two days after the election and promised to search for "common ground," but a broad charm offensive by White House officials seemed unlikely. "They're not in the mood for it, and they don't think it would work," said a close Bush adviser.

The weeks leading up to the election had been bitter for Bush. The last time control of Congress was up for grabs in a midterm election, it seemed Republican candidates across the country couldn't see enough of—or be seen enough with—the popular President. In the closing five days of 2002, Bush swooped through 17 cities, garnering cheers from tens of thousands of voters who packed tarmacs and arenas from Aberdeen, S.D., to Blountville, Tenn.

This midterm election also turned out to be all about Bush, but it was a much lonelier experience for him. He still filled smaller rooms, especially the kind where people were willing to write five-figure checks for the privilege of dining with a Republican President. And he was welcomed warmly in places where having local reporters point out Bush's difficulties provided a diversion from the candidate's own.

But when Air Force One touched down in tightly contested congressional districts in 2006, it often turned out that the G.O.P. candidate there had discovered a previous commitment elsewhere, the political equivalent of suddenly needing to have your tires rotated. Yes, Florida Congressman Clay Shaw ran radio ads to boast of his record of working closely with a President, but the one he was talking about was Bill Clinton. When a conservative commentator asked Bush to give him some good news, the President replied, "You're talking to Noah about the flood."

The campaign trail wasn't the only place where Bush watched his friends scatter. In the weeks before the election, only 38% of Americans said they still believed his invasion of Iraq was a good idea, and 61% said they didn't think he had a clear plan for handling the war. But Bush has lived by the political philosophy that when the crowd is against you, you just strut more boldly across the stage. That's why he held a news conference 13 days before the election to hug his war policy even tighter—and went on to claim to a group of reporters gathered at the White House on Nov. 1 that Rumsfeld would serve out the rest of the President's term. That promise lasted only some 18 hours after the polls closed.

This time around, the President stayed up until after 11 on Election Night, long past his usual bedtime, to watch as Republican dominion over Washington fractured and slipped away on a tide of voter anger about Iraq and dissatisfaction with the direction of the country. Both he and his inner circle had been publicly buoyant to the end, and aides had said the boss planned to make "lots" of congratulatory phone calls. Instead, he wound up talking to New York Republican Representative Tom Reynolds, who barely kept his seat after taking some of the blame for the House leadership's handling of the Mark Foley page scandal.

What if Washington does become a stage for sectarian conflict after Nov. 7? For one thing, most of Bush's legislative agenda could be bound for gridlock. White House officials still talk hopefully of expanding Bush's No Child Left Behind education legislation. Other issues for which they argue they could get some kind of bipartisan cooperation include moving toward energy independence, lowering health-care costs and fighting terrorism with new tactics. Bush's advisers even talk of enlisting Democrats for some grand push for entitlement reform, although anything like Bush's disastrous effort to add private accounts to Social Security would seem out of the question, given his inability to get anywhere on the issue even with a Republican Congress.

Where can the lame duck in the White House get traction? One area in which the President and a Democratic Congress might be able to make common cause is the immigration bill that has been one of his signature issues. The Senate has gone along with Bush's comprehensive approach, which includes both tougher enforcement of the border and expanded access to legalization for immigrants who are already in this country. But the closest thing to an immigration policy to be approved by House Republicans was a 700-mile "vir-

tual fence" along the border—a politically expedient idea that, enacted on its own, left Bush with less to horse-trade in his efforts to get what he really wants, which is serious reform.

In his White House press conference, the President repeatedly used the phrase "fresh perspectives" to describe Rumsfeld's resignation and his past two years in office. Yet for Bush, the new viewpoints may come from some very old hands indeed. As he ramped up his drive to intervene in Iraq in 2002, the younger Bush firmly rejected the counsel of his father's inner circle, including former National Security Adviser Brent Scowcroft. He allowed Vice President Dick Cheney and Rumsfeld to drive another trusted member of his father's team, General Colin Powell, out of his post as his first-term Secretary of State. Yet Gates, the President's new Pentagon chief, is an old family hand who ran the CIA under President George H.W. Bush. And James Baker, whom the younger Bush charged with chairing the Iraq Study Group in March, served the senior Bush as Secretary of State and is considered the consigliere of the Bush dynasty.

In a fascinating Oedipal drama, the younger Bush seemed at last to be turning to his father's trusted inner circle for guidance. The 43rd President has two more years to leave his mark on history. If he can call on wise counselors for fresh perspectives and reach out across the bitterly partisan divides he has helped manufacture in American society, he will have delivered, six years later, on his campaign promise to unite, rather than divide, his nation. ∎

LAST LAP: The President waves to supporters as he lands in Cincinnati, Ohio, on Sept. 25 to campaign for incumbent Republican Senator Mike DeWine; on Nov. 7 Ohio voters soundly rejected the G.O.P. candidate

Capitol Offenses

Bribes, boys and brouhahas: official misdeeds send Americans' trust in federal legislators to new lows. Here's a scorecard of the year's scandals

"FOLLOW THE MONEY" AND "LOOK FOR THE GIRL" USED TO be the two guiding principles of reporters investigating political corruption. In 2006 both mottoes proved prescient—except that the girl turned out to be a gaggle of teenage boys working as congressional pages. Throughout the year, Americans were staggered by a steady stream of stories detailing the fiscal and moral corruption that stalked the halls of the U.S. Capitol. Congressmen on the take, Congressmen on the make: by the fall, polls showed Americans' respect for Congress was at its lowest ebb in years.

Those pursuing the trail of monetary corruption found it led from disgraced lobbyist Jack Abramoff to more than a dozen members of Congress and into the White House itself (the lobbyist raised more than $100,000 for President George W. Bush's 2004 re-election bid). Nor was Abramoff alone in playing with tainted cash. Republican House members Curt Weldon of Pennsylvania and Bob Ney of Ohio were also investigated, as was Democrat William Jefferson of Louisiana. California Republican Randy Cunningham resigned the House and is serving prison time for accepting bribes.

In September the scandal involving Florida Republican Mark Foley's inappropriate come-ons to teenage male House pages threatened to remove House Speaker Dennis Hastert of Illinois from his post. As the November elections made clear, Republicans who had swept into power in both houses of Congress in 1994 by pledging to clean up the capital city's culture of corruption failed to keep their own House clean— so voters stepped in and did it for them. ∎

Jack Abramoff

The powerful G.O.P. lobbyist was known for playing host to influential guests at his four luxury skyboxes at major sporting arenas; for comping their meals at his upscale restaurant, Signatures, and for flying them aboard private jets to all-expenses-paid golf outings in Scotland. But Abramoff pleaded guilty in January 2006 to felony counts stemming from two separate federal investigations. The first, based in Washington, arose from his fraudulent dealings with casino-owning Indian tribes. He billed several of them a total of $82 million, while he and his partner, Michael Scanlon, exchanged e-mails referring to them as "idiots," "troglodytes" and "monkeys." He once billed a Texas tribe that was trying to get approval to reopen a casino while he also secretly lobbied on behalf of another client to prevent the casino from reopening.

Abramoff's second guilty plea, in Miami, dealt with conspiracy and fraud in his purchase, in 2000, of a Florida company that operated a fleet of gambling boats. Along with half a dozen former colleagues who have also pleaded guilty, Abramoff is now believed to be helping federal prosecutors delve further into his murky affairs. One casualty of that probe was Ohio Republican Congressman Bob Ney, who pleaded guilty in October to taking bribes from Abramoff. For weeks Ney declined to resign his seat; he finally yielded to pressure from senior Republicans and stepped down four days before the election.

A House in Need of a Scrub

Public esteem for Congress plummeted in 2006, as multiple revelations and charges about wrongdoing by elected officials, their aides and the lobbyists with whom they do business came to light. The politician who fell the furthest was House majority leader Tom DeLay, who announced in April that he would not seek re-election to Congress and resigned from his seat two months later. The Texas Republican continues to insist that he will be vindicated on the state charges he faces, predicts he will not be implicated in the Abramoff probe and says he plans to continue to work for conservative G.O.P. causes in retirement.

TOM DELAY: The embattled politician known as "the Hammer" left Congress in June, two days after a second of his former aides pleaded guilty and announced that he was cooperating with federal prosecutors investigating disgraced lobbyist Jack Abramoff. Delay also remains under indictment in Texas, where state prosecutors have charged him with money laundering, an allegation he describes as politically motivated.

RANDY (DUKE) CUNNING- HAM: After pleading guilty in November 2005 to multiple counts of conspiracy, mail fraud, wire fraud and tax evasion, the decorated former Navy fighter pilot was sentenced in March to eight years in prison and ordered to pay $1.8 million in restitution. Later that month, the Treasury Department auctioned off home furnishings and antiques the California Republican had received as bribes.

WILLIAM JEFFERSON: The FBI raided the Capitol Hill office of the eight-term Louisiana Democrat on May 20 (a 2005 search of his Virginia home had turned up $90,000 in a freezer). In an unusual show of bipartisan outrage, House Republicans denounced the FBI foray as unconstitutional. Jefferson, who had not been formally charged as this book went to press, denied any wrongdoing and faced a tight race for re-election in November.

A Speaker Under Fire

Soon after the Sept. 29 resignation of Republican Mark Foley over his improper contacts with congressional pages, the scandal spread to senior House leaders. Most vulnerable was House Speaker Dennis Hastert of Illinois, who initially said he first learned of Foley's misconduct only when it became public, in September 2006.

The Speaker's claims were undercut when two G.O.P. Congressmen claimed that Hastert had been advised of the issues surrounding Foley's behavior at least six months before his improper e-mails became public. Hastert back-tracked, saying he did not "explicitly recall" these conversations but did not dispute that they took place. That admission led to a chorus of calls for the Speaker's resignation. Hastert refused to resign, and President Bush stood by him. In the wake of the sweeping Democratic victory in the House on Nov. 7, the Speaker said that he would give up his post as leader of his party in the chamber.

Iraq: Still Searching For the Way Forward

The U.S. intervention in Iraq bogs down amid sectarian violence, as a new coalition government is unable to stabilize the ravaged nation

HISTORIANS MAY SOMEDAY RECALL 2006 AS A MILESTONE year, a Janus-like tipping point in which the U.S. came as close as it ever would to achieving the Bush Administration's mission of transforming the state once run by strongman Saddam Hussein into a stable democracy—even as Americans also began to acknowledge that the U.S. mission, as originally conceived, was unlikely to succeed.

Optimists pointed to signs of real progress. Under U.S. guidance, Iraqis finally put together an elected coalition government, which trained, equipped and deployed more than 300,000 security forces. The long process of holding Saddam accountable for his crimes continued: a death sentence was handed down in November at his first trial (for reprisals conducted in the town of Dujail after a 1982 assassination attempt) even as a new trial began, focusing on the deadly campaign he waged against the Kurds in the late 1980s. In June, the most dangerous terrorist in Iraq, al-Qaeda's Abu Mousab al-Zarqawi, was killed in a U.S. strike.

Yet pessimists pointed to a steady drumbeat of bad news that provided a host of reasons to be gravely concerned about U.S. prospects in Iraq. The February bombing of the Askariya mosque, the holiest site in Iraq for the country's majority Shi'ite population, brought the nation to the brink of civil war between Sunnis and Shi'ites. Throughout the year, sectarian violence relentlessly escalated. By July, a United Nations study concluded that Iraqi civilians were dying at the pace of more than 100 each day, an increase of more than 77% over the death rate in 2005. The following month, General John Abizaid, the U.S. military's top commander in the region, acknowledged to a Senate panel that sectarian violence in Iraq had grown so strong that civil war was a distinct possibility. Meanwhile, the U.S. military suffered further erosion of its reputation thanks to a series of murders and rapes allegedly committed by its troops.

On the domestic front, disaffection among Americans grew steadily. By August a TIME poll showed that 63% of those surveyed disapproved of President George W Bush's handling of the war, while more than half believed that it was hurting U.S. efforts to combat terrorism. By October even Bush was conceding at least the perception of parallels between Iraq and Vietnam, and the White House announced that it was dropping the rhetorical theme "stay the course."

In Iraq, facts on the ground continued to outpace decision makers in Washington. In late October, Shi'ite cleric Muqtada al-Sadr's Mahdi Army brazenly (albeit briefly) seized control of the southern city of Amarah, bringing the country another step closer to outright civil war. The following month, an army of 80 gunmen, dressed in police uniforms, stormed into the Ministry of High Education in a daylight raid and abducted more than 150 people. In the November mid-term congressional elections, Americans rendered their verdict on the Administration's handling of the war. With a resounding vote of "no confidence," they handed control of Congress to the Democratic Party. The departure of Defense Secretary Donald Rumsfeld followed immediately. When his replacement, former CIA chief Robert Gates, was asked during Senate confirmation hearings whether he thought the U.S. was winning in Iraq, Gates answered, "No, sir."

Gates' candid answer directly contradicted the frequently stated Administration position that the U.S. was on course to succeed, if slowly, in its mission to bring democracy and stability to Iraq. His view was seconded in the same December week by a bipartisan panel chartered by Congress to assess the U.S. position in Iraq. In a long-awaited report, the Iraq Study Group—chaired by Republican former Secretary of State James Baker and former Democratic House member Lee Hamilton of Indiana—called the situation there "grave and deteriorating." In its unanimous finding, the 10-member group issued 79 recommendations for U.S. action in the shattered nation, including a gradual withdrawal of troops that would send the vast majority of Americans in Iraq home by early 2008, and a U.S. diplomatic outreach to other key nations in the region, including Syria and Iran. The President quickly signaled that he was unlikely to pursue either course and said that he would rely on a series of other position papers due to be issued late in 2006 before putting in place a policy that would offer "a way forward" in Iraq. On one point, however, few disagreed: with 144,000 U.S. troops in harm's way in the increasingly unstable land, a way forward—or a way out—was long overdue. ∎

VIGILANT: Members of the U.S. Army's 1-14 Cavalry, 3rd Stryker Brigade combat team patrol the southern Doura district of Baghdad on Aug. 7, 2006

A Coalition Government Is Born, But Is Iraq Ready for Democracy?

Few politicians owe as much to another country's government as Nouri al-Maliki does to the Bush Administration. In April, strong U.S. backing catapulted al-Maliki into his job as Iraq's Prime Minister after a two-month impasse over the nomination of his predecessor, Ibrahim al-Jaafari. Sunni and Kurdish politicians say U.S. Ambassador Zalmay Khalilzad leaned heavily on them to back al-Maliki. "Khalilzad made it clear there was only one man on Washington's wish list," a senior Kurdish leader told TIME on condition of anonymity. "Al-Maliki cannot have any doubts about why he got the job."

But Iraq's new PM could be forgiven for harboring doubts about why he wanted it. Ayad Jamaluddin, a member of Iraq's Parliament, describes al-Maliki's task as trying "to pilot a plane in which every single passenger has a different destination." The government reflects the divisions of Iraq's population: al-Maliki and one of the nation's two Vice Presidents, Adel Abdul Mahdi, are Shi'ites. President Jalal Talabani is a Kurd. The other Vice President, Tariq al-Hashimi, is a Sunni. Such is the fractious state of Iraqi politics that even members of al-Maliki's own Shi'ite bloc often disregard him, while Kurd and Sunni leaders are openly hostile.

Al-Maliki spent his first months in office promising to pursue Sunni insurgents with "no mercy" and to crush Shi'ite militias "with an iron fist." The first boast has been mostly made good on, albeit in ways he never intended. Death squads dressed in Iraqi security uniforms routinely round up groups of Sunnis and execute them. (Whether these killers are disguised or are actual government security forces, which are known to be heavily infiltrated by Shi'ite partisans, is much debated.) But the vow to crack down on the competing Shi'ite militias that are waging open warfare (against each other, Sunnis and Americans) in Iraq's streets was a nonstarter, undermined from the beginning by the fact that the Prime Minister's own party is closely tied to powerful Shi'ite groups that command the very militias he says he wants to crush, such as the Mahdi Army controlled by powerful Shi'ite cleric Muqtada al-Sadr. The strength of al-Maliki's Shi'ite ties was underscored in Septem-

IN THE MIDDLE: New Prime Minister Nouri al-Maliki meets with George W. Bush in Baghdad, above, in June; and with fellow Shi'ite Mahmoud Ahmadinejad in Tehran, right, in September

ber, when he visited Iran and conferred with President Mahmoud Ahmadinejad, leading some critics to complain that Iraq's Prime Minister has closer ties to Tehran than to Washington.

By October, Iraq's Parliament had begun to consider proposals for decentralizing the country's government, giving the regions dominated by Sunnis, Shi'ites and Kurds semiautonomous status. But for all the discord, there is one point on which a majority of Iraqis seem to agree. A poll conducted by the U.S. State Department and made public in September showed that 65% of Iraqis surveyed favored an immediate U.S. pullout. Those in the minority, who hope for a longer-term U.S. presence, seem to consist primarily of Iraqi's Kurds, whose long history of persecution has ended under U.S. occupation, and Sunnis, who are increasingly under siege from Shi'ite-dominated militias and security forces.

For his part, al-Maliki seemed less concerned with long-term strategy than short-term survival. And he appeared ready to declare his independence from Washington, if that was the price required. In late October, when two top U.S. officials in Iraq, General George W. Casey Jr. and Ambassador Khalilzad, announced that the Iraqi government had accepted timetables for the roll-out of political reforms, al-Maliki reassured his Shi'ite following in Iraq that he had not accepted them and would not bend to pressure by the U.S. government in managing Iraq's internal affairs.

In November, relations between al-Maliki and Bush were further strained when the Iraqi abruptly canceled a scheduled meeting with the President and King Abdullah II of Jordan in Amman. The snub came a day after a memo written by Bush's National Security Adviser, Stephen Hadley, was leaked to the press; it described the Prime Minister as isolated and ineffectual. The two men did hold a shortened meeting in Jordan, and Bush termed his counterpart "the right guy for Iraq." But al-Maliki's position resembles that of his troubled nation: he may be a hostage to forces he cannot control. ∎

In the Year's Bloodiest Fighting, Iraqis Battle Iraqis

On Feb. 22, 2006, the Askariya Mosque in Samarra, the holiest Shi'ite shrine in Iraq, was blown apart by a bomb. In response, the radical Shi'ite cleric Muqtada al-Sadr sent his private militia, the Mahdi Army, on the warpath against Iraq's minority Sunnis, believed to be responsible for the blast. The violence took its worst toll in and around Baghdad. For much of the year the Sunnis, led by al-Qaeda in Iraq chief Abu Mousab al-Zarqawi, responded in kind, staging a wave of suicide bombings and terrorist attacks that massacred thousands of Shi'ites.

The change in the bloodletting in Iraq was telling. Once driven by anti-Americanism—the Mahdi Army fought pitched battles against U.S. troops in 2004, and al-Zarqawi initially directed his insurgency against foreign occupation forces—both sides were, by 2006, more intent on killing one another. While Shi'ite militias were fired by a determination to avenge centuries of Sunni oppression, al-Zarqawi branded Shi'ites as betrayers of the faith and called for their liquidation, stoking a sectarian war within Islam that led to a year of bloodshed. Though al-Zarqawi was killed in a U.S. air raid on June 6, the tempo of the sectarian violence never let up; estimates of the death count in the struggle reached the tens of thousands.

To further complicate matters, especially from the U.S. perspective, neither faction is monolithic. On the Shi'ite side, al-Sadr's Mahdi Army often clashes with the Badr Organization, a rival militia with close ties to Iran that controls Iraq's Ministry of the Interior. The ministry's many thousands of security forces are often loyal to the Badr group, whereas local police units in Shi'ite-dominated areas are heavily infiltrated by Mahdi Army members. Officials from both camps refuse to interfere with (and sometimes even join) marauding gangs that have killed or kidnapped thousands—not only Sunnis but also Shi'ites who don't subscribe to their radical version of the faith. At first Iraq's government ignored allegations of the alliance, suggesting that the victims were deceived by insurgents masquerading as police or soldiers. By the fall of 2006, however, Prime Minister Nouri al-Maliki's government began to acknowledge that at least some elements of the security forces had gone rogue.

Caught in the middle of these swirling currents were U.S. troops, who launched a new campaign in August, Operation Forward Together, intended to restore order in Iraq's capital. By October, however, U.S. Major General William B. Caldwell IV called the persistence of ruthless sectarian violence in Baghdad "disheartening" and acknowledged that the effort to take back the city had gone nowhere. In some respects, the shift in focus on the part of Sunni insurgents and Shi'ite militias—from killing coalition forces to violence against fellow Iraqis—may be a grim portent for what is to come. "They absolutely think we're leaving," retired Marine Colonel Thomas X. Hammes, told TIME in August. "This is what happened in Afghanistan when it became clear the Russians were leaving. The factions began fighting each other." ∎

DESTROYED: The golden dome and much of the rest of the Askariya Mosque lies in ruins in Samarra, north of Baghdad. The bombing of the shrine sacred to Shi'ites touched off a furious round of sectarian violence in Iraq

PROOF? This photo is alleged to show bloodstains in a civilian home in Haditha, where Iraqi residents charge U.S. Marines killed innocent women and children

Did U.S. Marines Massacre Civilians in Haditha?

The outfit known as Kilo Company, 3rd Battalion, 1st Marine Regiment, wasn't new to Iraq in 2005, when it moved into Haditha, a Euphrates River farming town about 150 miles northwest of Baghdad. Several members of the unit were on their second tour of Iraq; one was on his third. The men in Kilo Company, veterans of ferocious house-to-house fighting in Fallujah, seemed prepared for the ordeal of serving in an insurgent stronghold like Haditha, the kind of place where the enemy attacks U.S. troops from the cover of mosques, schools and homes and uses civilians as shields, complicating Marine engagement rules to shoot only when threatened. In Haditha, says a Marine who has been there twice, "you can't tell a bad guy until he shoots you."

Yet as TIME first reported in March 2006, some members of Kilo Company may not have attempted to distinguish between enemies and innocents in autumn 2005. At about 7:15 a.m. on Nov. 19, a string of four U.S. humvees was on routine patrol in a residential area when a white taxicab approached from the opposite end of Hay al-Sinnai Road. The Marines made hand and arm signals for the taxi to stop. But as the car halted near the first humvee, a bomb under the fourth one exploded, killing its driver, Lance Corporal Miguel (T.J.) Terrazas, 20, of El Paso, Texas, wounding two of his comrades and shattering windows 150 yds. away. Marines later said the convoy almost immediately began to take fire from several houses on either side of the road. Locals disputed that account, claiming the only firing after the explosion was done by the Marines.

Suspecting that the four young men in the taxi either triggered the bomb or were acting as spotters, the Marines ordered the men and the driver, who by then had exited the taxi, to lie on the ground. When they ran instead, the Marines shot and killed them. Witnesses claimed that after gunning down the five men, a few members of Kilo Company moved through four homes along nearby streets, killing 19 others, including five women and four children, over the next five hours. The Marines disagree, contending they took small-arms fire from at least one house. But as TIME's story detailed in March, only one of the 24 victims was found with a weapon. (The military's initial report stated that Terrazas and 15 civilians were killed in a roadside blast and that shortly afterward the Marines came under attack and returned fire, killing eight insurgents.)

Two official investigations into the events at Haditha are ongoing: one into the deaths, and one into an attempted cover-up that may have followed. Some of the most disturbing elements of the story were confirmed in May, when members of Congress who were briefed on the military probes disclosed that at least some members of the Marine unit may be charged in connection with the deaths of the Iraqis. The charges could include murder, which carries the death penalty. John Murtha, the top Democrat on the House Defense Subcommittee, who initially backed the war but later emerged as a vocal critic of the Bush Administration's handling of it, said U.S. Marines were guilty of murdering civilians, adding, "It's much worse than was reported … there was no firefight." Staff Sergeant Frank D. Wuterich, the Marine who was the unit leader in Haditha on Nov. 19, told TIME in August that he had not participated in a cover-up of the incident; he also said he intended to file a civil lawsuit for defamation of character against Murtha.

Like the Abu Ghraib prison scandal before it, Haditha threatens to become one of the war's signature debacles, an alleged atrocity committed by a small group of service members that comes to symbolize the enterprise's larger costs. And like Abu Ghraib, Haditha may not be the last tragedy of its kind. In July, the Army filed charges against a recently discharged private for allegedly raping a 15-year-old Iraqi girl in March 2006, then murdering her, both of her parents and her 7-year-old sister. ∎

The Top Terrorist in Iraq Is Eliminated at Last

Within a farmhouse set back in a grove of date palms amid the fertile, fruit-growing countryside just outside Baqubah, 30 miles north of Baghdad, Abu Mousab al-Zarqawi relaxed with friends over dinner on June 6. Then, around 6:12 p.m., two 500-lb. bombs crashed through the roof of the cinderblock building, killing or mortally wounding everyone inside, including al-Zarqawi, the leader of al-Qaeda in Iraq, who for three years had been the single most powerful terrorist in the lawless, reeling nation.

With his use of videotaped beheadings, spectacular suicide bombings that killed hundreds of Iraqis at a time and Houdini-style escapes from U.S. pursuers, the Jordanian-born al-Zarqawi had become the face of the Sunni insurgency in Iraq, complete with a $25 million bounty on his head. President Bush had paid the terrorist the perverse compliment of referring to him more than 100 times in speeches, charging him with wanting to "sow as much havoc as possible" and "destroy American life."

The bombs were dropped by F-16 Fighting Falcons, called in by U.S. special forces operatives who had been trailing al-Zarqawi for months. After the bombs hit, the terrorist managed to hold on briefly, mumbling and struggling as he died in the ruins on a stretcher brought by soldiers. The news of his death gave the Bush Administration's Iraq policy a much needed if short-lived bump in U.S. opinion polls, but al-Zarqawi's foreign fighters represented only a sliver of the bad guys in Iraq. Intelligence estimates sug-

THE END: On June 7, a U.S. spokesman announces the death of the most prominent terrorist leader in Iraq

gest he commanded a few hundred men, of whom only a fraction were foreign jihadis. By most estimates that's less than 5% of the 25,000 to 50,000 insurgents believed to be operating inside the country.

Even as Iraqi officials trumpeted "the beginning of the end of al-Qaeda in Iraq," al-Zarqawi's successor was named. A U.S. military spokesman identified him as Egyptian-born Abu Ayyub al-Masri, who uses the nom de guerre Abu Hamza al-Muhajer. U.S. and Iraqi forces have been hunting al-Qaeda's new kingpin in Iraq ever since. ∎

STRUGGLING: U.S. soldiers take cover as a CH-47 Chinook helicopter takes off in the Helmand province in southern Afghanistan on June 18, 2006

The Other War: The Taliban Comes Back in Afghanistan

The year 2006 in Afghanistan marked a turning point in the battle for the nation's future: U.S. and allied troops handed over command of peacekeeping and security duties to NATO's International Security Assistance Force (ISAF). It also brought a worrisome resurgence of the land's former rulers, the Taliban. By year's end, the number of foreign peacekeeping troops in the restless nation had been beefed up to approximately 40,000 (almost four times the level at the end of 2005), but the challenges the international force faced in stabilizing a nation one-third larger and 15% more populous than Iraq were still enormous.

In good news, the capital city of Kabul remained secure and the elected government of U.S.-backed President Hamid Karzai was still in power. Around the country, more than 5 million children attended school; 25% of them were girls, who were denied schooling by the Taliban. The size of the country's economy has tripled in the past five years. Support from NATO countries remains solid: there's a consensus in Europe that Afghanistan isn't Iraq; the war there is considered both legal and necessary to keep the nation from reverting to being a safe haven for the Taliban and al-Qaeda.

The more ominous news: much of the economic growth is based upon a record opium harvest, and the countryside outside of Kabul still belongs to regional warlords, some of them Taliban sympathizers, others loyal to the highest bidder. The resurgent Taliban now fields platoon-sized units of about 40 men or more and is using tactics honed by insurgents in Iraq, including suicide attacks and roadside bombs. An estimated 1,000 Taliban fighters, as much as one-fifth of their total strength, were killed in September's Operation Medusa. In October NATO's ISAF commander, Britain's General David Richards, predicted that the first six months of 2007 would be a turning point. "If we fail to deliver on the promises that they [the Afghans] feel have been made to them," he said, "increasing numbers will say, 'Listen, we want you to succeed, but we can't wait forever.'" ∎

NationNotes

A Misfire for the Vice President

In one of the more curious news stories of recent years, Vice President Dick Cheney, an avid hunter, fired a shotgun blast into the face of a friend, attorney Harry Whittington, 78, while they were hunting quail at a Texas ranch on Feb. 11. The White House did not reveal the accident until almost 24 hours after it occurred, and the incident was first made public in a local newspaper story.

Whittington recovered, but Cheney (here, hunting in 2002) became a target himself—of endless gibes, puns and jests aimed by TV comics, editorial cartoonists and bloggers.

A Port Deal Burns the White House

The Bush Administration found itself politically isolated after it was revealed in February that it had signed off on a deal in which the management of six major seaports in the U.S. would be sold to DP World, a company based in the United Arab Emirates and owned by the government of Dubai. President Bush argued strongly for the deal but ended up at odds not only with Democrats but also with congressional leaders of his own party—and with voters. Polls showed a wide majority of Americans opposed the deal, which was quietly nixed early in March.

A Kidnapped Journalist Weathers an Ordeal

Freelance U.S. journalist Jill Carroll, 28, was reporting in Iraq for the *Christian Science Monitor* when she was kidnapped in Baghdad by masked gunmen on Jan. 7 while en route to a scheduled interview with a Sunni politician. Carroll's interpreter, Allan Enwiyah, was shot dead. Ten days later TV network al-Jazeera showed a silent 20-sec. videotape of Carroll; an accompanying message demanded the release of all female Arab prisoners being held by coalition forces in Iraq—or Carroll would be executed. Two later videos showed Carroll wearing Islamic dress and pleading for her life. U.S. authorities refused to heed the kidnappers' demands, and Carroll was released unharmed on March 30.

In a follow-up video that was soon released, Carroll is seen praising the insurgents in Iraq; she maintained the statements were the price for her release and branded her captors "criminals."

> **"** It's the young crowd—20-, 30- and 40-year-olds—who are coming back and making things happen in New Orleans … There is so much work to do. **"**
>
> —DIANE RAGAN,
> *Realtor in New Orleans*

New Duo for National Security

On Nov. 8, when President George W. Bush announced Defense Secretary Donald Rumsfeld's resignation, he said he would appoint Robert M. Gates, 63, a widely respected former head of the CIA, to replace him. Gates, above, sailed through Senate confirmation hearings in December, as legislators were eager to establish new leadership at the Pentagon. Gates will work with a new CIA chief: after Porter Goss step-ped down as head of the intelligence agency in May, the Senate approved Bush's choice for the post, Air Force General Michael Hayden, the deputy director of National Intelligence.

The Big Not-So-Easy

New Orleans struggled to find its footing in the first full year after Hurricane Katrina breached its levees and flooded its streets in late August 2005. In February the streets of the historic and beloved city filled with revelers for the famed Mardi Gras parades, right. In May controversial mayor Ray Nagin, 50, overcame a challenge from Mitch Landrieu, scion of a famed Louisiana political family, to retain his post.

A TIME report on the city's status showed an uneven, halting recovery, with some sections still devastated and far from coming back to life, while in others, land speculators were buying up entire blocks at a time in hopes of profiting from the city's eventual renaissance. In good news, the city was spared a storm this year

Moussaoui: Life in Prison

After legal proceedings that dragged on for years, Zacarias Moussaoui, 38, the only person ever to be tried for complicity in the deadly terror attacks of 9/11, pleaded guilty to conspiracy and was sentenced by a Virginia jury to six life terms of imprisonment with no possibility of parole. The verdict and sentencing put an end to a frustrating case that led many observers to question the sanity of the French citizen of Moroccan descent: Moussaoui had chosen to represent himself and had repeatedly changed his account of his alleged ties to al-Qaeda.

A Needless, Heedless Tragedy in Kentucky

On the morning of Aug. 27, a regional jet flying as Comair Flight 5191 crashed while taking off from Blue Grass Airport in Lexington, Ky., killing all 47 passengers aboard, as well as two of the three crew members. The airplane had been assigned to take off from Runway 22, routinely used for jets of this size, but the pilots had instead used Runway 26, far too short for the plane to take wing. The error was so obvious as to be easily noticed from the airport's control tower, but after clearing the craft for takeoff, the lone controller in the tower turned to other duties and did not visually observe the takeoff. The Federal Aviation Administration (FAA) later declared that it had violated its internal policies calling for two controllers to be present in the tower. Federal agencies were still probing the events as of Nov. 1, 2006.

World

"When you give ... people a chance to express themselves at the polls and ... they're unhappy with

A Stunning Win for Hamas in Palestinian Elections

The Bush Administration's hopes of spreading democracy in the Middle East encountered a severe bump in the road when voters went to the polls in the Palestinian Legislative Council elections on Jan. 25 and handed a landslide victory to the radical Hamas Party, which took 76 seats in the 132-seat Parliament. The moderate ruling Fatah Party, led by Palestinian Authority President Mahmoud Abbas, the successor to Yasser Arafat, won only 43 seats; 13 went to fringe parties. Here, Hamas supporters in Gaza celebrate their victory. Hamas, long a force for aggression among Palestinians, has refused to renounce violence and recognize Israel's right to exist. In response, the U.S. and Israel cut off payments promised to the Palestinian Authority under the 1993 Oslo Accords, putting a long-sought settlement to Israeli-Palestinian tensions once again seemingly out of reach.

the status quo, they'll let you know." —President George W. Bush, following the Hamas victory

Iran's Immoderate Voice

MAHMOUD AHMADINEJAD IS A PRESident unlike any Iran has known since its 1979 revolution: belligerent, naive, at once a fundamentalist and nationalist. In only his first year in office, he has risen out of obscurity to become one of the most outspoken and noteworthy leaders in the world.

Elected by a razor-thin margin in 2005, Ahmadinejad, 49, has failed to deliver on promises to fix Iran's economy. But his incendiary rhetoric—he has declared the Holocaust a "myth," said Israel should be "wiped away" and called the Jewish state "a stain of disgrace"—has made him the most polarizing head of state in the Middle East. His uncompromising stand on Iran's right to enrich uranium has increased the threat of future turmoil in the region and edged the U.S. and his nation closer to a military confrontation. And the $300 million he sends each year to support Lebanon's Hizballah militants paid off when his proxies successfully resisted a summer onslaught by Israel.

The leader's deeds outrage Iran's many moderates, yet the former mayor of Tehran and Revolutionary Guard commander has formulated a message that most Iranians agree with: the time has come for their land to be strong again. He has made nuclear power an issue of national pride, and so far, his position that the U.S. "can't do a thing" has proved true. His May 2006 letter to President George W. Bush, proposing negotiations, rattled the White House.

In 2006 Ahmadinejad diverted eyes from Iran's economic woes and turned his figurehead office (Supreme Leader Ayatullah Ali Khamenei holds the real power) into a bully pulpit. Whether Iran's quest for nuclear weapons succeeds or is thwarted by a U.S. military strike or is only an elaborate bluff, one thing is clear: Ahmadinejad is making the world a more complicated—and possibly more dangerous—place. ■

Mahmoud Ahmadinejad

"The people of the United States are also seeking peace, love, friendship and justice." —Ahmadinejad, in a TIME interview

Hugo Chavez

"I sting those who rattle me. So don't mess with me, Condoleezza." —Chavez, in a radio broadcast

The Caustic Caudillo

"THE DEVIL CAME HERE YESTERDAY," VENEZUELAN PRESI-dent Hugo Chavez assured the United Nations General Assembly in September, adding of President George W. Bush's address the day before, "he came here talking as if he were the owner of the world." A sniffing Chavez went on to claim that the podium still reeked of sulphur. While U.S. audiences are unused to such histrionics, a growing constituency within Venezuela, throughout Latin America and around the world reveled in Chavez's performance.

Chavez's rise is a lesson in what can happen when the U.S. disses an entire continent. After 9/11, when most Latin American nations refused to endorse the U.S. invasion of Iraq, Bush testily turned his back on the region—but not before he was widely accused of backing a failed 2002 coup against the Venezuelan President, his loudest critic south of the border. The White House denies the charge, but the perception of U.S. bullying won Chavez international sympathy, and his anti-U.S. rhetoric has been soaring ever since; he won a new six-year term in office in December.

Meanwhile, U.S. influence in Latin America is perhaps at its lowest ebb in decades. As the Bush Administration cuts development aid to the area, Chavez, 52, who controls the hemisphere's largest oil reserves, is giving cash-strapped neighbors discounts and favorable financing on Venezuelan oil as well as billions of dollars in loans. That largesse, coupled with the region's distrust of globalization, is aiding a surging leftist mood in South America, which propelled Chavez ally and former U.S. nemesis Daniel Ortega to power in a November election in Nicaragua.

Portraying himself as the David who will put the brakes on Bush's imperialist Goliath, Chavez strutted his way through a meeting of nonaligned nations in Havana in September. His growing ties to another oil-rich U.S. gadfly, Iran's President, Mahmoud Ahmadinejad, have prompted U.S. Secretary of State Condoleezza Rice to brand Chavez a threat to hemispheric stability. He was pleased: after all, goading Uncle Sam—and Aunt Condoleezza—has been a successful formula for the provocative President. ■

Hassan Nasrallah

"No army in the world will be able to make us drop the weapons from our hands!" —Nasrallah

The New Hero of the Arab Street

SANDWICHED BETWEEN A PAIR OF BRUISERS PREPARED TO take a bullet to protect his life, Sheik Hassan Nasrallah lives in the crosshairs. Yet by the standards of Arab strongmen, Nasrallah is a charmer. In TV appearances, the leader of Lebanon's Hizballah Party appears more soothing than bellicose. There is none of Saddam Hussein's finger wagging or the late Yasser Arafat's eye-bulging lectures or Osama bin Laden's hectoring, haughty sneer. Instead, Nasrallah reads deliberately from notes, every so often looking into the camera and flashing a smile.

Nasrallah has led the Shi'ite "Party of God" since 1991 and has paid a price; his eldest son was killed by Israeli forces in southern Lebanon in 1997. Although he said after the summer war in southern Lebanon between Hizballah and Israel that "had we known that the kidnapping of the soldiers would have led to this, we would definitely not have done it," he appears to have profited from the conflict. Nasrallah, 46, staked a claim to being the most popular leader in the Arab world by surviving Israel's aerial on-slaught and fighting its army to a standstill, and by insisting that the ransom for the Israeli soldiers Hizballah abducted in July include not only Lebanese prisoners closely linked to Hizballah but also several jailed Palestinian militants. The sheik thus cast himself as a statesman and the custodian of Muslim honor. He is also the only Arab leader in history who can credibly claim to have won a military victory over Israeli forces; he led a merciless guerrilla campaign that persuaded Israel to quit a decades-long occupation of southern Lebanon in 2000.

After claiming victory in the 2006 conflict, Nasrallah set out to win the peace. As the August cease-fire went into effect, the sheik went on TV to promise that Hizballah would give $10,000 to those whose homes were damaged and that the party would help rebuild the homes. (With more than $300 million in annual aid coming from Iran, he can afford this kind of generosity.) Within days, Nasrallah's aides had dispatched a corps of engineers to survey war-torn areas, its members wearing Hizballah yellow vests and matching baseball caps whose logos read JIHAD OF CONSTRUCTION. Now that's p.r., Nasrallah-style. ■

Man in the Middle

"HOPE OVER FEAR," IRAQ'S PRIME Minister, Nouri al-Maliki, proclaimed in a July 26 address to a joint session of the U.S. Congress. "Liberty over oppression ... Let there be no doubt: today Iraq is a democracy." But while the rhetoric tried to soar, the reaction among al-Maliki's audience was distinctly earthbound. "Is he living in Iraq?" asked Florida Congresswoman Debbie Wasserman-Schultz. Al-Maliki is truly a man in the middle: he was appointed in April to head Iraq's new government chiefly because he was the person least objectionable to both Washington's and Iraq's various feuding parties. He has the near impossible task of repairing the damage wrought by three years' worth of poorly considered policies and half-measures, some instituted by U.S. officials and generals who have long since gone home, others by Iraqi politicians now discredited.

Al-Maliki, 56, is an unlikely candidate to be charged with unifying his fractious nation. His previous job as spokesman for the Islamic Dawa Party, headed by his predecessor, Ibrahim al-Jaafari, earned him a reputation as a Shi'ite partisan. When he took office, he was completely unknown to most Iraqis. A backroom politician plainly ill at ease in public, al-Maliki is an ornery figure with little natural charisma. Still, he managed to gain the trust of Sunni leaders during the tortuous 2005 negotiations over Iraq's constitution, when he helped cobble together a compromise with Sunni and Kurdish groups. But a September 2006 trip to Tehran to meet with a fellow Shi'ite, Iranian President Mahmoud Ahmadinejad, raised new questions about his ability to unify Iraq's house divided. ∎

Nouri al-Maliki

"We're impressed by your courage ... and we're impressed by the courage of the Iraqi people." —President George W. Bush

Bombs over Lebanon

Seeking to take out a longtime foe, Israel attacks the militant Hizballah Party. But the mini-war ends in a stalemate, leaving Lebanon battered

THE MODERN MIDDLE EAST IS A CONSTANT FOUNT OF conflicts. And like any of the other crises that have rocked the region in recent years, the mini-war that broke out in southern Lebanon in July 2006 can't be understood without a history lesson—and a scorecard to identify the players, both apparent and hidden, who were vested in its outcome. The story begins with Lebanon, which played the role of man in the middle in the struggle—and paid a steep price for it. A province of Syria until the early 20th century, Lebanon is one of the most Westernized nations of the Middle East, thanks to its large minority of Christians, its lo-

cation on the Mediterranean, its trading heritage and the two decades it spent after World War I as a protectorate of France. Lebanon's capital, Beirut, with its lively sidewalk cafés, splendid beaches, seaside Corniche and jet-set tourist crowd, has long been known as the Paris of the Middle East.

But Lebanon also borders on the state of Israel, the "Zionist entity" so deeply hated by its Arab neighbors. For decades now, Arab terrorists operating out of southern Lebanon have staged raids and fired mortar shells into northern Israel, denying the Israelis peace of mind. In the early 1980s, the terrorists operating out of Lebanon were controlled by Yasser

BANG! Israeli soldiers brace themselves from the shock wave of their artillery fire as they bombard Hizballah positions in southern Lebanon on July 14

Arafat's Palestine Liberation Organization (P.L.O.). After Israel's Ambassador to Britain, Shlomo Argov, was shot in cold blood and seriously wounded by the Palestinian terror group Abu Nidal in London in 1982, fed-up Israelis sent tanks and troops rolling into Lebanon to disperse the guerrillas. But when a group of Lebanese Christians sympathetic to the Israelis, the Phalangists, massacred Arab women and children living in a refugee camp outside Beirut, the pressure of world opinion sent most Israeli forces back across the border. Yet some troops stayed in place in a "security zone" in southern Lebanon that served as a buffer between the two nations.

Arafat's P.L.O. group was driven out of Lebanon, but a new group eventually took its place: Hizballah, the "Party of God." This militant group is a Shi'ite fighting force, founded and bankrolled by Shi'ite Iranians, who are not Arabs but Persians. Under Sheik Hassan Nasrallah, its leader since 1991, Hizballah warriors made life so miserable for Israeli troops in the southern security zone that Israel unilaterally withdrew from the area in 2000, a tacit admission that the price of maintaining the zone was too high. Hizballah has also become a major player in Middle East politics, using the estimated $300 million it receives annually from Iran to burrow more deeply into

SHARDS: The Haret Hreik neighborhood of Beirut, a Hizballah stronghold, lies in ruins on July 20 after heavy Israeli air strikes

the social fabric of Lebanese life. It has become not only a militant group but also a social organization and political party with deep roots in Lebanon's society, a state within a state. Nasrallah also burrowed deeper into the ground, building stronger bunkers in the landscape of southern Lebanon and stockpiling rockets and mortars to be deployed in a future battle with Israel.

That battle arrived in the summer of 2006. Predictably, the conflict began not in Lebanon or Israel but in the Palestinian territories administered by Israel, long the sparkplug for Arab-Israeli conflicts. Regional tensions escalated early in June after seven members of a Palestinian family died in a Gaza beach explosion, which Palestinians blamed on an errant Israeli artillery shell. On June 25, in response, guerrillas from the militant Palestinian Hamas Party tunneled under the border between Gaza and Israel and kidnapped Israeli corporal Gilad Shalit, 19. A spiral of violence had been triggered: Israel next bombed bridges and roads inside Gaza and destroyed six transformers at the central power plant, cutting off electricity to 45% of the territory's inhabitants.

Enraged by these attacks on fellow Arabs, Hizballah now entered the fray. On July 12 members of the group crossed the border into Israel, killed eight Israeli soldiers and took two more soldiers hostage. Ehud Olmert, who had served as Israel's Prime Minister for only six months following a January stroke that felled Ariel Sharon, acted vigorously. The untested new PM quickly declared the taking of the hostages "an act of war" and ordered air attacks on Hizballah positions in Lebanon—1,000 sorties in the first 24 hours—as well as limited ground incursions.

Olmert's robust response appeared to be aimed not only at

punishing Hizballah but also at reshaping Israel's neighborhood, reducing Hizballah's strength until it could no longer pose a threat to the Jewish state. Olmert's Cabinet backed his policy, agreeing it was time to hit back, hard, to demonstrate that Israel was willing to fight. The message was aimed at both Hizballah and Iran.

Yet to Israel's surprise—and eventual dismay—Hizballah didn't look for a way out. Instead, it launched an escalation of its own, shooting longer-range missiles than it ever had before into Israel, forcing some 1 million Israelis in the north of the country—a sixth of the nation's population—either to evacuate their homes or hunker down in bomb shelters.

> **"This is the Israeli army. We are about to increase our military operations in south Lebanon, and you are advised to leave immediately ..."**
> —Anonymous phone message received by Lebanese community leaders

In the weeks that followed, Israeli aircraft and artillery pummeled Beirut. At one point, Israeli forces dropped 23 tons of bombs on a bunker in the capital city where they believed Nasrallah was hiding; he survived. On July 22, Israel escalated the conflict, sending 2,000 troops and tanks across the border to invade Lebanon; at the conflict's peak, some 10,000 Israeli troops were in Lebanon. Yet it appeared that Israel was doing more damage to Lebanese civilians and infrastructure—and to its own reputation—than to Hizballah.

Israel's strategy was complicated by the fact that Hizballah functions as a political party and has a representative in the Lebanese Cabinet. The Lebanese government and army are too weak to take on the group and its patrons. As hundreds of thousands of Lebanese fled their homes and northern Israelis languished in bomb shelters, Israel took a beating in the court of world opinion. Critics charged its response was far out of proportion to the initial provocation. Meanwhile, Hizballah portrayed its survival as a major victory—and that opinion was shared by an unexpected source, the Israeli public. A strong majority of Israelis had supported Olmert's aggressive strategy early on, but as the war escalated with little good news to report, more and more Israelis began to regard it as a mistake, and Olmert's grip on power was threatened.

As in any Middle East conflict, the aftershocks from the battle in Lebanon soon spread to the U.S. and the U.N. Nations around the world pressured Israel and Hizballah to arrange a cease-fire. On Aug. 11, following intense international diplomacy and several visits to the region by U.S. Secretary of State Condoleezza Rice, the U.N. Security Council approved Resolution 1701, which called for a cease-fire. Under its terms, Hizballah agreed to disarm, Israel agreed to withdraw its troops from Lebanon, and a force made up of Lebanese troops and U.N. peacekeepers would be sent to patrol a buffer zone between Lebanon and Israel. France, Spain and Turkey were among nations committing troops to the U.N. force. On Aug. 15, Israeli troops began withdrawing from Lebanon; most had left by Aug. 25.

Amid Lebanon's ruins, a war for hearts and minds now took shape. Having survived the war, Hizballah mobilized to win the peace: Nasrallah went on TV to promise that the Party of

ANGUISH: A man carries a dead girl from the ruins of Qana in Lebanon. More than 50 people were killed when Israeli planes bombed the suspected hotbed of Hizballah militants on July 30

God would give $10,000 to all Lebanese whose homes had been damaged. The funds came directly from Tehran. On the other side of the fence, the Saudis, concerned by the rising power of Arab militant groups not only in Lebanon but also in Iran and Iraq, provided $1 billion in funds to Lebanon's central bank and $500 million more to help the rebuilding effort. It will be some time before the fallout of the battle can be assessed, but at first blush the summer's events seemed a clear victory for Nasrallah and Hizballah and a setback for Olmert and Israel. And the biggest loser of all was the one group that appeared to have no dog in this hunt: the battered citizens of Lebanon, stuck in the middle again. ∎

Voices in the Storm

Like a stone tossed in a pond, events in the Levant ripple outward to affect the interests of nations around the region—and around the world. The U.S. is involved in the area not simply because it is the world's sole superpower, but because it also has a unique relationship with Israel, the region's only Western-style democracy, and is committed to guaranteeing its security. Iran and Syria are also deeply involved in the affairs of Lebanon, with Iran supporting its fellow Shi'ites in the Hizballah Party and Syria supporting Hizballah as the enemy of Syria's enemy, Israel. At right, the leaders involved in the summer battle state their positions.

Ehud Olmert

"The decision to launch the war . . . is entirely mine. I know that there is controversy about the degree, the extent of our success . . . One thing is very clear. In Beirut and in other capitals in the Middle East, it has been understood that we do not ignore any offense and attack on our sovereignty, our citizens, our civilians and our soldiers."
—Speech, 8/28/06

Hassan Nasrallah

"I know what they say in their closed rooms. They say that Hizballah left this war hurt and injured. That is stupid. Stupid. The Israelis are saying that Hizballah has still retained the largest part of its military capabilities . . . It is true that we were fighting in a true war, but we won a historic, strategic battle."
—Al-Jazeera interview, 9/12/06

Mahmoud Ahmadinejad

"Are the Lebanese inside the occupied lands right now, or is it the other way around—that the Zionist troops are in Lebanese territory? Lebanon is defending its independence. We are not at all happy with war. That is why on the first day we condemned these recent conflicts and we asked for an immediate cease-fire."
—60 Minutes interview, 8/13/06

Condoleezza Rice

"A cessation of hostilities will take place so that there can't be a return to the status quo ante, which is ... important to all of the parties because we don't want to create a situation in which we get out of this and then you create the conditions in which Hizballah, a state within a state, goes across the line again, abducts soldiers and we get another war."
—Press conference, 8/6/06

Nuclear Tremors in Asia

After years of threats, North Korea successfully tests an atom bomb, and the United Nations clamps down with sanctions that could lead to talks

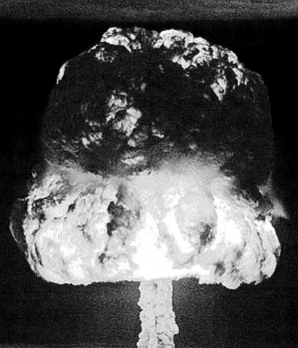

FEAR THIS: The U.S. tested nuclear bombs on Bikini Atoll in the South Pacific during the late 1940s and '50s; this 1954 test provided an iconic image of the power of nuclear weapons. Fifty-two years later, North Korea tested its first nuclear device, lending new urgency to antiproliferation efforts

NUCLEAR WORLD

A defiant North Korea has now become the ninth country on earth to have the Bomb. President Bush has said the U.S. "will not tolerate" a nuclear North Korea, but containment may be the only viable option remaining

Sources: Carnegie Endowment for International Peace; Natural Resources Defense Council

Countries with nuclear weapons; Nuclear Nonproliferation Treaty (NPT) signatories

Countries with nuclear weapons; not NPT signatories

Countries with the ability to develop nuclear weapons

U.S.

Argentina, Brazil, Chile

South Africa

Britain

France

Iran
Suspected program

Israel
Unconfirmed arsenal

Pakist

THE RUMBLE OUT OF THE FAR NORTH OF THE PEOPLE'S Democratic Republic of Korea was, in some ways, unremarkable. It registered a mere magnitude 4.2, the equivalent of a light earthquake. "More fizzle than pop," said a U.S. intelligence source dismissively—but it was a fizzle heard around the world. Defying urgent pleas and intense pressure from the rest of the world, North Korea successfully tested a nuclear bomb on the morning of Oct. 9 at a site near the city of Kilju in country's northeast, about 250 miles from the capital, Pyongyang. The test moved the issue of North Korea's nuclear capability into a tense new phase.

For more than a decade, the U.S. and North Korea's deeply concerned neighbors in east Asia—South Korea, Japan, China and Russia—had worked to get Pyongyang to abandon its nuclear ambitions. But the so-called six-party talks with Pyongyang chugged to a standstill in July 2006, after the U.S. cracked down on illegal North Korean bank accounts maintained in the Chinese city of Macau.

The world responded quickly to the successful nuclear test. Led by the U.S., on Oct. 15 the United Nations Security Council passed tough sanctions against the rogue nation, calling for an embargo on the shipment of any goods or materials that could be used in its missile and nuclear programs, as well as inspections of cargo entering and leaving the country to ensure enforcement. The sanctions also severely limited the flow of luxury goods into the nation, a measure aimed not at its starving millions but at its leader Kim Jong Il, whose fondness for the best things in life is well documented.

The robust sanctions may have done the trick. On Oct. 31, in Beijing, diplomats from China, North Korea and the U.S. announced the first glimmer of good news from the peninsula in more than a year: the North Koreans had agreed to rejoin the talks. The news came only a day after the top U.S. general in South Korea warned that Kim Jong Il would probably conduct further nuclear and missile tests before the end of the year. Christopher Hill, the chief U.S. representative at the six-party meetings, told reporters in Beijing that talks could resume "in November or possibly December" and that Pyongyang had reaffirmed its commitment to a preliminary agreement that had been reached.

While Hill said that North Korea had made no pledge to refrain from further nuclear tests, Japan's conservative Foreign Minister, Taro Aso, reportedly said that Tokyo opposes resuming the talks unless Pyongyang agrees to renounce its weapons program. But North Korea is unlikely to surrender a bomb it spent decades and millions building, before talks even begin. When—and if—North Korea does return to the bargaining table, it's possible that the relatively solid coalition cobbled together by the U.S. in the aftermath of the success-

Careful Where You Point That Thing, Mr. Kim!
The man whose finger is on North Korea's nuclear trigger, Kim Jong Il, 65, is utterly unpredictable. Since taking over from his father Kim Il Sung in 1994, the "Dear Leader" has allowed millions of his people to die of starvation, even as he indulged a penchant for brandy and mistresses and funneled millions into his frantic pursuit of a nuclear weapon. After the U.S. protested when North Korea test-fired seven ballistic missiles in July, Kim called U.S. Secretary of State Condoleezza Rice "a political imbecile." Foreign Minister Kim Gye Gwan declared, "What I hear is big brothers saying to little brother, 'Don't do that,' but we are not a little boy. We have nuclear weapons." Above, Kim is seen swaggering on Japanese TV after the test.

ful test could easily break down, as China and South Korea reduce the pressure they put on Pyongyang even as the U.S. and Japan maintain a hard line.

The resumption of the talks, however, represents a diplomatic win for China, which had been forced to take the central role in reining in its wayward ally Pyongyang. It was China's decision to support the U.N. sanctions that gave them teeth, and Chinese envoys made repeated trips to Pyongyang in October. The message was clear: North Korea had embarrassed Beijing by testing a nuclear device despite repeated warnings by the Chinese against doing so. By at least agreeing to return to the six-party talks, Kim appeared to be preventing a loss in international face for his status-conscious friends in Beijing. The fact that China's rival Japan had begun making noises about the possibility, however remote, of starting its own nuclear program undoubtedly added to the pressure on North Korea.

The real test will be how all six parties react once the talks resume—assuming, of course, the talks do resume in 2006. It's best to mark your calendar in pencil when you're dealing with North Korea. ∎

The U.S. and Russia control most of the world's nuclear warheads. Those stockpiles are shrinking, but other countries are pursuing nuclear weapons

Russia

China

North Korea
Testing weapons

Indonesia,

Deployed nuclear weapons, in thousands

U.S.

Others

40

30

20

10

0

U.S.S.R./Russia

1950 1960 1970 1980 1990 2000

Estimated nuclear stockpiles, 2005

Russia
8,800 inactive 7,200 deployed

U.S.
10,315

Russia has about 8,800 warheads in reserve or awaiting dismantling

In addition to the known nuclear powers, North Korea says it has nuclear weapons. Iran could be next

Est. warheads

	Est. warheads
China	410
France	350
Britain	200
Israel	100-170
India	75-110
Pakistan	50-110
North Korea	Unknown

Iran Dreams Of Grandeur

Roused by a provocative President, a nation demands nuclear power

WHEN IRAN'S PRESIDENT, MAHMOUD AHMADINEJAD, sat down for an exclusive interview with TIME's Scott MacLeod in September 2006, he took pains to praise the U.S. "My general impression is that the people of the United States are good people ... [they] are also seeking peace, love, friendship and justice." The implication of that "also": Ahmadinejad's Iran was a fellow traveler on the Peace Train. But those who believed that contention hadn't been paying attention. For hard-liners in Iran, the U.S. has been the "Great Satan" since the days when Ayatullah Ruhollah Khomeini held 52 Americans hostage for 444 days. And under the rabble-rousing Ahmadinejad, Iran has continued to demonize the U.S., as government-approved protesters march through the streets chanting "Death to America!"

Yet that's not what is most worrisome about Iran. Here's what is: over the past decade, Iranians have acquired many of the pieces, parts and plants needed to make a nuclear device. Although its officials insist that Iran's nuclear ambitions are limited to producing energy, the regime has asserted its right to develop nuclear power and enrich uranium that could be used in bombs as an end in itself—a symbol of sovereign pride, not to mention a useful prop for politicking.

Ahmadinejad crisscrossed his country in 2006, making Iran's right to a nuclear program a national cause and trying to solidify his base of hard-line support among the Revolutionary Guard. The pursuit of nuclear power is popular with average Iranians and the élites as well. "Iranian leaders have this sense of past glory, this belief that Iran should play a lofty role in the world," Nasser Hadian, professor of political science at Tehran University, told TIME.

The West has been unable to compel Iran to halt its suspicious nuclear program. The Bush foreign policy team, now led by Secretary of State Condoleezza Rice, has done more diplomatic work on Iran than on any other project in its 5½ years in office. For more than 18 months, Rice has kept the Administration's hard-line faction at bay while leading a coalition that includes four other members of the United Nations Security Council— Britain, France, China and Russia—

"DEATH TO AMERICA": Iran's fiery President, Mahmoud Ahmadinejad, claimed in an interview with TIME that he is a good friend of the U.S., but government-sanctioned street rallies in Tehran and other Iranian cities depicted the U.S. and Israel as criminal states. Above, the Israeli flag is burned in a demonstration. At left, the President visits one of Iran's estimated 18 to 30 nuclear facilities; he insists Iran wants nuclear power for peaceful uses

whose goal is to convince Iran to dial back its nuclear dreams.

Yet these diplomatic efforts are moving too slowly, some believe, to stop the Iranians before they acquire the makings of a nuclear device. And Iran has played its hand shrewdly so far. Tehran took weeks to reply to a June 1, 2006, formal proposal from the U.N. Security Council calling for a halt to uranium enrichment. When it did, its official response was a mosaic of half steps, conditions and boilerplate that suggested Tehran has little intention of backing down.

Meanwhile, Ahmadinejad caught the Bush team off-guard by sending a rambling 18-page letter to the U.S. President in May, in which he asked for direct U.S.-Iran talks over Iran's nuclear intentions and praised Jesus Christ and Christianity but condemned Israel and U.S. support for the Jewish state. The White House did not reply, nor did it respond to an even more grandstanding follow-up by Iran's President, who volunteered to appear in a globally televised debate with Bush. The two diplomatic sallies, whether whimsical or serious, seemed to succeed in their propaganda goals: to present Ahmadinejad as Bush's equal in stature and to make the White House look defensive, inflexible and unresponsive. "The Iranians," a Western diplomat in Washington told TIME, "are very able negotiators." Even, it seems, with those who share their search for love, peace, friendship and justice. ∎

Terrorists Hit Bombay

Muslim extremists are arrested after seven bombings strike railways in India's bustling financial and cultural center, killing more than 180 people

MANGLED: Police officers probe the wreckage of a commuter railway car in the hours after the bombing. Suspicion immediately centered on militant Islamic groups that had successfully staged previous deadly terrorist strikes in India

INDIA TODAY—POLARIS

O NE OF THE GREAT STORIES OF RECENT YEARS HAS BEEN the emergence of India as a major new player on the global stage—a phenomenon TIME noted in a cover story on "India Inc." in June 2006. One beneficiary of the nation's renaissance has been the city of Bombay, also known as Mumbai: it is now a global financial capital at the heart of the fast-growing Asian economy and a popular destination for foreign investment. Yet in today's world, such success can also attract those invested in spreading horror: on July 11 terrorists struck the city's transportation system. In the span of 11 minutes, seven bombs ripped through the packed first-class carriages of commuter trains in Bombay during the morning rush hour. The explosions split the carriages open and hurled passengers onto the tracks. Bruised and bloodied, many made it to hospitals. Many others who were in the centers of the carriages ended up in the morgue. More than 180 innocent people were killed and more than 700 wounded in India's worst terrorist attack since 1993.

In the aftermath of the bombs, Bombay's people showed resilience and bravery—just as did those in Madrid, London and New York City in similar circumstances. Within hours of the explosions, police were combing through the wreckage for clues. Days later, they released the names of three suspects, and the focus of the investigation settled on Lashkar-e-Toiba (LeT), a militant Islamic group based in Pakistan. LeT was suspected of working in concert with indigenous Indian Muslims from the banned Student Islamic Movement of India (SIMI).

The two radical groups were previously accused of detonating eight bombs in Bombay in late 2002 and 2003, killing 70 people. Lashkar-e-Toiba, meaning "Army of the Pure," has fought Indian rule in Kashmir since the early 1990s. Largely funded by Pakistan's Inter-Services Intelligence agency in the 1990s, LeT was designated a foreign terrorist organization by the U.S. in 2001. The group was subsequently banned by Pakistan, but it has nevertheless been implicated in several attacks on Indian government buildings and in a 2006 massacre of non-Muslim villagers in Kashmir. Both LeT and SIMI denied any involvement with the bombings in Bombay, telling news agencies that "Islam does not permit the killing of innocents." But by the end of September, Indian police had arrested more than a dozen suspects from the two groups.

India is home to the world's second largest Muslim population. But in a nation of more than 1 billion, they are still a disadvantaged minority and often the target of discrimination. A mounting sense of persecution among young Muslims in India, combined with high unemployment and mounting anxiety about what many see as a global crusade against their religion, makes fertile recruiting ground for homegrown groups such as SIMI. Police raids, detentions and the oft-reported abuses that occur under such detentions only add to their sense of being unfairly targeted.

Days after the bombings, Indian Prime Minister Manmohan Singh linked the bombings to Pakistan, and in the fall Indian authorities said they would present evidence tying the bombings to the neighboring nation's spy agency. Tortuous peace talks between the two countries now seem all the more challenging, as the long conflict between Hindus and Muslims on the subcontinent heats up once again. ∎

WorldNotes

Gone Fishin'

In the Palestinian territories, membership in a militant party is routine. But to American eyes, it's still jarring to see a masked member of the Hamas Party, whose appeal to Palestinians continues to grow, stroll along a Gaza beach, just another passing pedestrian.

A Swift Military Coup in Thailand

Daily demonstrations in Bangkok in the spring nearly forced Thailand's Prime Minister, Thaksin Shinawatra, to step down, as Thais accused the billionaire of corruption and nepotism; his get-tough policy in the nation's largely Muslim south was also unpopular. On Sept. 20 the army stepped in, sending tanks into the streets, above, to topple the regime peacefully—shortly after Shinawatra addressed the U.N. on the topic "The Future of Democracy in Asia."

Fidel Castro: Conflicting Health Reports

Rumors that Cuba's President, Fidel Castro, 80, had died hit the Internet in July, but authorities in Cuba insisted that Castro had merely undergone abdominal surgery and would make a full recovery. Below, Venezuela's incendiary President, Hugo Chavez, joins Fidel's brother and longtime right-hand man Raúl, 75, to demonstrate a bedside show of support. But U.S. officials told TIME early in October they are now convinced that Castro is suffering from terminal cancer and will never return to power. Contacted by TIME, Cuban officials strongly denied the reports.

A Furor over Cartoons

In September 2005 a Danish newspaper published cartoons caricaturing Islam's Prophet Muhammad. The cartoons attracted little attention until their existence was denounced early in 2006 by Muslim leaders; artistic depictions of Muhammad are regarded as anathema within Islam. A global furor erupted, as Muslims assailed not only the offending illustrators but also French newspaper editors, Norwegian diplomats, U.S. troops in Iraq, the state of Israel and peddlers of Danish food. Mobs in Damascus torched the Danish and Norwegian embassies; rioters set fire to the Danish consulate in Beirut; Iranians hurled gasoline bombs at Denmark's embassy; effigies were burned in Pakistan, above. The events seemed a bellwether of a deepening divide between Western societies, with their free-speech traditions, and Islam.

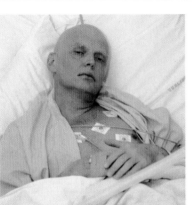

Death by Poison in London

The Nov. 23 death of former KGB spy Alexander Litvinenko in London opened a window into a murky world of Russian political intrigue. Tests proved that Litvinenko had been poisoned, just as he had claimed. The toxin in his system was the very rare radioactive isotope polonium-210, which requires a nuclear reactor to cook up and specialized training to handle. Soon other people close to Litvinenko in his final days also tested positive for the substance.

Before his death, Litvinenko named Russian President Vladimir Putin (of whom he had been a relentless and bitter critic) as the engineer of his murder, describing him as "barbaric and ruthless." The Kremlin denied the charge in the strongest terms. Litvinenko's murder, coming on the heels of other recent deaths among Putin's political enemies, sent a subzero chill over Russia's already frosty civil society. Multiple investigations in a number of countries were ongoing as this book went to press.

> " We are all willing to sacrifice ourselves. We are calling for the death of Jews and Christians. "
>
> —QASI NAZIR, *20, a Muslim student marching in Afghanistan to protest cartoons of Muhammad*

New Woes in Somalia

Lacking a central government for 15 years, Somalia has become a patchwork of fiefdoms run by murderous warlords. In June guerrillas (above) from the Islamic Courts Union (ICU), a radical Islamist group, took over the capital, Mogadishu. Hard-liners in the ICU pushed aside moderates and appointed as their head a man the U.S. suspects of collaborating with al-Qaeda.

The Leaderboard, 2006 Edition

Power changed hands in nations around the world in 2006, as well as at the U.S.-based organization that seeks to unite the nations. The longest goodbye will belong to Britain's long-serving PM Tony Blair, who declared he would resign his post by September 2007.

STEPHEN HARPER, CANADA
Conservative Harper, 47, won a surprising victory in January, ending the Liberal Party's 12 years in power. Although born in Toronto, he is a man of the west who has been a strong voice for Alberta.

TONY BLAIR, BRITAIN
The beleaguered Labor PM, 53, has long been out of favor for his support of the U.S.-led intervention in Iraq. Under pressure, Blair said he would step down and planned to cede power in the party to long-time rival Gordon Brown.

SHINZO ABE, JAPAN
Elected in September to replace outgoing PM Junichiro Koizumi, Abe, 52, is Japan's first PM to be born after World War II. One goal: to mend his nation's currently strained relations with the People's Republic of China.

FELIPE CALDERÓN MEXICO
The right-wing Calderón, 44, eked out a tight win over left-leaning Andrés López Obrador. The vote was so close that the winner was not announced until four days after voters went to the polls in July.

ROMANO PRODI, ITALY
The center-left Union coalition led by "Il Professore," a former academic, won a narrow victory over controversial PM Silvio Berlusconi's coalition in April. Prodi, 67, had previously served as Italy's PM (1996-98).

BAN KI-MOON, UNITED NATIONS
The Foreign Minister of South Korea was elected in October to replace outgoing U.N. Secretary General Kofi Annan. The longtime diplomat, 62, is regarded as an expert on rogue state North Korea.

TIME PERSON OF THE YEAR

You.

THE "GREAT MAN" THEORY OF HISTORY IS USUALLY ATTRIBUTED TO THE Scottish philosopher Thomas Carlyle, who wrote that "the history of the world is but the biography of great men." He believed that it is the few, the powerful and the famous who shape our collective destiny as a species. That theory took a serious beating this year.

To be sure, there are individuals we could blame for the many painful and disturbing things that happened in 2006. The conflict in Iraq only got bloodier and more entrenched. A vicious skirmish erupted between Israel and Lebanon. A war dragged on in Sudan. A tin-pot dictator in North Korea got the Bomb, and the President of Iran wants to go nuclear too. Meanwhile nobody fixed global warming, and Sony failed to make enough PlayStation3s for the holidays.

But look at 2006 through a different lens and you'll see another story, one that isn't about conflict or great men. It's a story about community and collaboration on a scale never seen before. It's about the cosmic compendium of knowledge Wikipedia and the million-channel people's network YouTube and the online metropolis MySpace. It's about the many wresting power from the few and helping one another for nothing and how that will not only change the world, but also change the way the world changes.

The tool that makes this possible is the World Wide Web. Not the Web that Tim Berners-Lee hacked together (15 years ago, according to Wikipedia) as a way for scientists to share research. It's not even the overhyped dotcom Web of the late 1990s. The new Web is a very different thing. It's a tool for bringing together the small contributions of millions of people and making them matter. Silicon Valley consultants call it Web 2.0, as if it were a new version of some old software. But it's really a revolution.

And we are so ready for it. We're ready to balance our diet of predigested news with raw feeds from Baghdad and Boston and Beijing. You can learn more about how Americans live just by looking at the backgrounds of YouTube videos—those rumpled bedrooms and toy-strewn basement rec rooms—than you could from 1,000 hours of network television.

And we didn't just watch, we also worked. Like crazy. We made Facebook profiles and Second Life avatars and reviewed books at Amazon and recorded podcasts. We blogged about our candidates losing and wrote songs about getting dumped. We camcordered bombing runs and built open-source software.

America loves its solitary geniuses—its Einsteins, its Edisons, its Jobses—but those lonely dreamers may have to learn to play with others. Car companies are running open design contests. Reuters is carrying blog postings alongside its regular news feed. Microsoft is working overtime to fend off user-created Linux. We're looking at an explosion of productivity and innovation, and it's just getting started, as millions of minds that would otherwise have drowned in obscurity get backhauled into the global intellectual economy.

Who are these people? Seriously, who actually sits down after a long day at work and says, I'm not going to watch *Lost* tonight. I'm going to turn on my computer and make a movie starring my pet iguana? I'm going to mash up 50 Cent's vocals with Queen's instrumentals? I'm going to blog about my state of mind or the state of the nation or the *steak-frites* at the new bistro down the street? Who has that time and that energy and that passion?

The answer is, you do. And for seizing the reins of the global media, for founding and framing the new digital democracy, for working for nothing and beating the pros at their own game, TIME's Person of the Year for 2006 is you.

Sure, it's a mistake to romanticize all this any more than is strictly necessary. Web 2.0 harnesses the stupidity of crowds as well as its wisdom. Some of the comments on YouTube make you weep for the future of humanity just for the spelling alone, never mind the obscenity and the naked hatred.

But that's what makes all this interesting. Web 2.0 is a massive social experiment, and like any experiment worth trying, it could fail. There's no road map for how an organism that's not a bacterium lives and works together on this planet in numbers in excess of 6 billion. But 2006 gave us some ideas. This is an opportunity to build a new kind of international understanding, not politician to politician, great man to great man, but citizen to citizen, person to person. It's a chance for people to look at a computer screen and really, genuinely wonder who's out there looking back at them. Go on. Tell us you're not just a little bit curious.

—By Lev Grossman

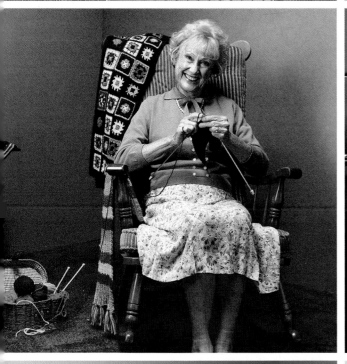

Power to the People

You control the media now, and the world will never be the same. Meet the decidedly diverse citizens of the new digital democracy

See the notorious "Macaca" clip by searching YouTube for "Sidarth"

S.R. Sidarth
The Accidental Assassin

HIS FULL NAME IS SHEKAR RAMANUJA SIDARTH. HE USUALLY goes by just his last name, or even just Sid. But most of the country knows him as "Macaca." Sidarth, 21, is a senior at the University of Virginia, majoring in government and engineering. He spent the past few summers doing campaign grunt work, and 2006 was no different. He worked for James Webb's Senate campaign, tracking Webb's opponent, Virginia Senator George Allen, videotaping his public appearances. On Aug. 11, the tracker became the tracked. Allen singled him out in the crowd with a long, rambling riff. "This fellow here, over here with the yellow shirt, Macaca or whatever his name is, he's with my opponent," Allen said. And later: "So welcome, let's give a welcome to Macaca here! Welcome to America and the real world of Virginia!" The clip is on YouTube. One copy has been played more than 320,000 times.

It's ironic that Allen would welcome Sidarth to Virginia, since Sidarth has lived there his whole life and Allen grew up in California. "He'd never addressed me before," Sidarth says, "and then to do so in this context—it was humiliating. That it was in a racial context made it worse." Later, some audience members went over to Sidarth to apologize.

It wasn't Sidarth's idea to put the clip on YouTube. "Getting drawn out into the limelight was really surprising," he says, and he means it. He's focused on keeping his head down and getting into law school. "Ultimately I'd hope people wouldn't pay as much attention to things like this, instead caring more about who can serve the country or the state better," he says. "Of course," he adds, "character plays into that. And this event reflected on Allen's character." ∎

Megan Gill
Generation Network

WHEN MEGAN GILL BROKE UP WITH HER BOYFRIEND IN NOvember, it wasn't easy, but she gritted her teeth and did the inevitable: she changed her relationship status on her Facebook page. "I knew there would be a flurry of annoying questions about what happened that I didn't want to answer," she says. "But it was the fastest way for it to be over and done with. Besides, if these people are supposed to be your friends, and care about you, then why keep it a secret?"

Gill, 22, a senior at the University of Portland, has a lot of friends—708, according to her Facebook page. Facebook is a social-networking website that does for today's teens and college kids what people used to do by gossiping and talking on the phone, but a lot more efficiently and publicly. You can post photos on your Facebook page, personal information, news about yourself, anything at all.

If you want to be Megan's friend, you're going to want to go through Facebook. She's a double major in special education and English, so she's busy, but she checks in with the site at least twice a day, often 10 times that. She'll post random updates to her profile just to let everyone know how she is: "Megan is so over first semester," "Megan is bummed about the election results." As she puts it, "Facebook is my generation's way of picking up the telephone." It also does things the phone can't. "If you want to organize something," Megan says, "it's much simpler to post a message on Facebook than leave 20 voice mails."

Social-networking sites can create and maintain relationships that wouldn't have existed otherwise. But is something lost in the process? "My friends and I are more in touch than was ever possible before," she says. "Older people had handwritten letters or called each other or whatever ... we have a much more convenient way of doing things." ∎

Gill with a few of her 708 Facebook pals

Watch video podcasters Waz and Lenny at *crashtestkitchen.com*

PAUL BLACKMORE FOR TIME

Waz and Lenny
The Un-Emerils

TO WATCH WARREN MURRAY, 34, AND LEANNE WHITE, 32, MAKE sponge cake is to hear the silent screams of Julia Child's dear, departed spirit. About 45 seconds in, they add two tablespoons of butter instead of two teaspoons, and it just goes downhill from there. Waz (as Warren is known) and Lenny (that's Leanne—it can be difficult to keep husband and wife straight) aren't professional chefs. They're copy editors at the *Guardian* newspaper in London. But their ham-fistedness in the kitchen is exactly what makes them great hosts.

Their show isn't a conventional cooking show. It's a video podcast called *Crash Test Kitchen*, and it's their sheer fallibility, their humanity, that makes the thing work. Waz and Lenny don't have the wizardly air of a Mario Batali or a Martha Stewart. "We have always tried to steer clear of the temptation to make it a Web version of a TV cooking show, with the old here's-one-we-prepared-earlier fakery and everything always turning out right," Waz says. Lenny says, "We try to be honest in our portrayal of cooking, so ordinary people feel brave enough to have a go at it." The sponge-cake episode is "probably the unintentionally funniest episode we've ever done," Waz says. "The thing was like trying to eat a sofa cushion." The episode ends with Waz furtively eating the ruined cake out of the trash. Even culinary daredevil Anthony Bourdain might have been scared to try that.

They don't sugarcoat the stresses of the marital kitchen either. "The bickering and disputes between Lenny and me seem to be part of the appeal," Waz says, "so we mostly leave that stuff in." The Web is a two-way medium, and their fans offer both culinary advice and unsolicited marriage counseling. One viewer called Lenny a "nagging housewife." ("I took it waaaay too seriously and was really cut up," she says.) Some viewers are even more assertive. "There have been some not-so-subtle come-ons towards Lenny," Waz says, "and we've been asked whether we will be filming future episodes in the nude." ■

Lee Kelley
The Bard of Camp Blue Diamond

CAPTAIN LEE KELLEY IS 35 AND HAILS FROM NEW ORLEANS. HE spent 12 years in the Army without being posted overseas, but that streak ended in June 2005 when he volunteered for service in Iraq and became a signal officer at Camp Blue Diamond in Ramadi. He has always been a writer—he has noodled around with a novel, done some freelance journalism. But it turns out he had to go all the way to Iraq to find his voice.

Kelley needed a way to convey to his family—especially his kids—what he was going through. As he puts it, "something I could leave behind if, God forbid, something happened to me." That's why he started taking some nonstandard gear with him on patrol: a notebook. "Work could last either eight hours or 20," he says. "I began to look forward to sitting down to write at the end of it." When he went off duty, he would grab a shower and then bang out a story about what had just happened. "Even though I was writing down what had happened in Ramadi that day," he says, "this was sort of an escape from the violence all around me."

Kelley is a military blogger, or mil-blogger, one of at least 1,200 servicemen and -women who write about their lives online. So far his blog, *Wordsmith at War*, has logged more than 200,000 hits. Mil-bloggers are a different breed from the domestic blogger who keeps, say, a record of his cat's mood swings. Here's Kelley on driving in Ramadi: "You have to go around big potholes and chunks of concrete blocking part of the lane. It's not a good feeling, because all your training tells you that these are ideal sites for IEDs ... The threat is very real, and you can sense it in the air. You can't think 'it won't happen to us,' you have to assume it will. Yet we discuss it in the same tone we might talk about last night's football game."

If Vietnam was the first war to be televised, Iraq is the first to be blogged—and YouTubed. Kelley says he and other soldiers are disappointed by how the media portray the conflicts in Iraq and Afghanistan. "If you looked at all the coverage, you'd think the whole thing is a huge mess waiting to blow up. I sometimes wonder where these reporters are. I guess it's not exciting enough to write about schools being built." Kelley and his fellow mil-bloggers aren't just writing letters to their families. Unlike generations of soldiers in the past, they're writing for history. "If they are archived, blogs will give the best account of this war," Kelley says. "No one knows what's going on better than the soldiers on the front lines." ■

Read Kelley's posts from Iraq at *wordsmithatwar.blog-city.com*

LANCE W. CLAYTON FOR TIME

"Blogs will give the best account of this war. No one knows what's going on better than the soldiers on the front lines. —Captain Lee Kelley

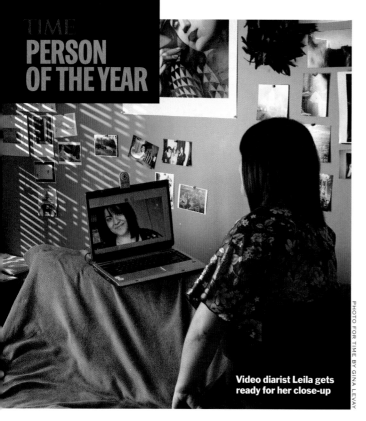

Video diarist Leila gets ready for her close-up

PHOTO FOR TIME BY GINA LEVAY

Leila

The Real Lonely Girl

LONELYGIRL15 IS ONE OF THE MOST VIEWED YOUTUBE USERS of all time. She's young and pretty, with a complicated and absolutely compelling personal life. She's also a work of fiction—lonelygirl15 was created by two professional screenwriters and an actress from New Zealand. But that doesn't mean there aren't real lonelygirls out there. Take Leila. She's 20 and lives in Maryland, where she's studying to be a social worker. Her personal life really is complicated. Online she describes her ethnicity as Middle Eastern—she's half Lebanese—and her religion as Muslim. She struggles with depression and her crush on the guy at the 7-Eleven. You know—complicated.

Like lonelygirl15, Leila—she doesn't give out her last name—is a video blogger. Leila has posted 49 videos on YouTube under the user name ppppanic (that's five *p*s). She speaks directly into her webcam about her life, her opinions, her shifting moods, what she did that day. She says *um* and *ah* a lot. She has been known to drink and blog. Sometimes she doesn't speak at all, just runs words across the screen while melancholy music plays in the background.

YouTube wasn't designed to be the public video diary of a generation of teens and twentysomethings. But sometimes the best inventions are the ones people find their own uses for. "You have people from all walks of life wanting to share a piece of their life with you," Leila says. "The feeling of togetherness is unbeatable. It's a beautiful thing."

Leila no longer even bothers with TV. "I think people are bored with the mainstream media. I've been so caught up in watching other people's videos. I find it more entertaining—much more real than the run-of-the-mill 'reality' show." Of course, in the post-lonelygirl15 era, there's always that question mark: How authentic are these faces on the computer screen? "I guess that's the only flaw," says Leila. "You can never really know the whole side of the story. You just get bits and pieces. You have to put blind faith in who the person is." ∎

Smosh

The Intertainers

ON NOV. 28, 2005, A VIDEO WAS UPLOADED TO YOUTUBE. IT shows two American River College students, Anthony Padilla and Ian Hecox, lip-synching to the *Pokémon* theme song. Their lip-synching is completely earnest. They're really into it. They're gonna catch 'em all. This video would go on to be viewed more than 17 million times. For six months it was the most watched video on all of YouTube. It's enough to shake your faith in a new medium.

Padilla and Hecox go by the joint nickname Smosh, and they are the *Saturday Night Live* of YouTube. Their videos are insanely popular. Their genius, if that's the right word for it, is in their unswerving, unwinking commitment to idiocy. It may also be in their shaggy haircuts. (*Smosh* is some kind of inside joke that has something to do with some friend of theirs talking about mosh pits . . . Never mind.) Since *Pokémon*, they have done other theme songs, including those for *Power Rangers* and *Mortal Kombat.* They have branched out into sketch comedy as well. (Typical setup: a friendly game of *Battleship* gone horribly, horribly awry.)

So far, Padilla and Hecox haven't been able to monetize their viral notoriety on any significant scale, although they do sell ads on Smosh.com. In fact, for Padilla and Hecox, being Internet celebrities is a lot like being normal people. "Our girlfriends hate that we're so busy," Hecox says. "The videos take up a lot of time, and we're working on several projects simultaneously. Overall, it really hasn't affected our lives." The dream is to end up like Andy Samberg (*Lazy Sunday*), who went from online comedy to the real *SNL.* But not everybody can live the dream, not even in the ultra-democratic YouTube era. "Our future is wide open," Padilla says. "There seems to be a huge potential in what we're doing, so we'll just keep doing what we're doing. And if nothing comes out of it—well, whatever." ∎

MARKHAM JOHNSON FOR TIME

Catch Padilla and Hecox by searching for "Smosh" on YouTube

Looking for Tila Tequila? Find her on *myspace.com*

BLAKE LITTLE FOR TIME

Tila Tequila
The Madonna Of My Space

TILA NGUYEN WAS 1 YEAR old when she moved to the U.S. from Singapore: she's Vietnamese by heritage and blond by choice. As for what she does for a living, there isn't really a word for it yet. Nguyen, 25, who goes by Tila Tequila professionally, is some combination of rapper, singer, model, blogger and actress. But what she mostly is is the queen of the vast social-networking website MySpace.

Nguyen—or, oh, fine, Tequila—may be the least lonely girl on the Internet. She has more than 1.5 million MySpace friends. Her profile on the site has been viewed more than 50 million times. Her self-published single, the profane and attitudinous *F___ Ya Man*, now playing on her MySpace page, has logged 13 million spins. (To listen to it is to hear the sound track of a million parents' dreams dying.) She gets somewhere from 3,000 to 5,000 new friend requests every day. She is something entirely new, a celebrity created not by a studio or a network but fan by fan, click by click, on MySpace.

Before she hit it big, Nguyen had posed for Playboy.com, modeled for car shows and auto mags and formed girl bands. But her big break came three years ago when MySpace founder Tom Anderson invited Nguyen over to his new site. She had spent plenty of time on websites like Friendster, but her outsize, confrontational personality kept getting her kicked off; Friendster booted her five times. "I joined MySpace in September 2003," Nguyen recalls. "At that time no one was on there at all. I felt like a loser while all the cool kids were at some other school. So I mass e-mailed between 30,000 and 50,000 people and told them to come over. Everybody joined overnight."

Nguyen clearly grasps the logic of Web 2.0 in a way that would make many CEOs weep. She sells Tila posters, calendars, a clothing line of hoodies and shirts. She has been on the cover of British *Maxim*. She has a cameo in a 2007 Adam Sandler movie. She has four managers, a publicist and a part-time assistant. It's hard to know how to read her rise: Does she represent the triumph of a new democratic starmaking medium or its crass exploitation for personal gain? Don't ask Tila—but she knows why it works. "There's a million hot naked chicks on the Internet," she says. "There's a difference between those chicks and me. They don't talk back to you." ∎

Harriet Klausner
The Constant Critic

WITHOUT THE WEB, HARRIET KLAUSNER WOULD BE JUST AN ordinary human being with an extraordinary talent. Instead she is one of the world's most prolific and influential book reviewers. At 54, Klausner, a former librarian from Georgia, has posted more book reviews on Amazon.com than any other user—12,896, as of this writing, almost twice as many as her nearest competitor. That's a book a day for 35 years.

Klausner isn't paid to do this. She's just, as she puts it, "a freaky kind of speed-reader." In elementary school, her teacher was shocked when Klausner handed in a 3½-hour reading-comprehension test in less than an hour. Now she goes through four to six books a day. "It's incomprehensible to me that most people read only one book a week," she says. "I don't understand how anyone can read that slow."

Klausner is part of a quiet revolution in the way American taste gets made. The influence of critics in print is on the wane: people don't care to be lectured by professionals on what to read, listen to or see. They're increasingly likely to pay attention to amateur online reviewers, bloggers and Amazon critics like Klausner. Such voices have a kind of just-plain-folks authenticity that professionals can't match. They're not fancy. They don't have an agenda. They just read for fun, the way you do. Publishers treat Klausner as a pro, sending her free books—50 a week—in hopes of getting her attention. Like any other good critic, Klausner has her share of enemies. "Harriet, please get a life," someone begged her on a message board, "and leave us poor Amazon customers alone."

Klausner is a bookworm, but she's no snob. She likes genre fiction: romance, mystery, science fiction, fantasy, horror. One of her lifetime goals is to read every vampire book ever published. "I love vampires and werewolves and demons," she says. "Maybe I like being spooked." Maybe she's a little bit superhuman herself. ∎

ANN STATES FOR TIME

Check out Klausner's book reviews at *snipurl.com/151kj*

It's incomprehensible to me that most people read only one book a week. —Harriet Klausner, Amazon.com's most prolific critic

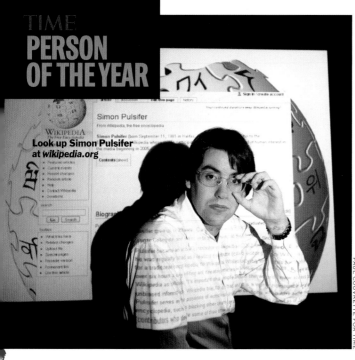

Look up Simon **Pulsifer** at *wikipedia.org*

PAUL COUVRETTE FOR TIME

Simon Pulsifer
The Duke of Data

THERE IS A LIST ON WIKIPEDIA OF WHO HAS WRITTEN OR EDITED the most entries, and for a long time the volunteer at the top of this list was a user known as SimonP. His real name is Simon Pulsifer. He is 25, unemployed and lives in Ottawa.

Pulsifer has written somewhere between 2,000 and 3,000 Wikipedia articles and edited roughly 92,000 others. "I've actually fallen to No. 2 in terms of edits," says Pulsifer, who's tall and a little overweight. "But it's a fairly meaningless measure, so I don't feel too bad." He first heard about Wikipedia in 2001, but it wasn't until 2003 that he got serious about contributing. That was the year he got a really, really boring summer job. At that point Pulsifer got "superinvolved" with Wikipedia.

Why would somebody donate so much of his time? "There's a certain addictive element," he says. Pulsifer was still in school, and writing Wikipedia entries turned out to be a handy way of studying for exams. While taking a Russian-history class, he wrote entries about the czars. He has chipped in pieces on African history and biblical studies. Some he wrote "off the top of my head." Others took research. "It's a combination of things," Pulsifer says matter-of-factly. "It's great to see your writing published online—it's not that easy to create things that are read by millions of people." He also liked the prestige that came with being a major player on Wikipedia. Granted, that prestige was mostly among other major Wikipedia players, but still.

Wikipedia isn't a paradise of user-generated content. It has plenty of errors in it, and omissions, although at this point it's considerably larger than the *Encyclopaedia Britannica*. Some people enjoy vandalizing it—erasing or falsifying entries. Earlier this year the entire staff of Congress was barred from Wikipedia for sabotaging one another's profiles. In a way it's as much a litmus test of human nature as it is a reference tool.

As for Pulsifer, he's quietly scaling back his compulsive Wikipediation. He no longer whizzes through 250 edits a day. "To a degree, I'm moving on," he says. He has had a couple of job offers; perhaps a well-paying gig will come along that will allow him to leave his parents' home, where he resides. No doubt a new Wikipedian will arrive to take his place. There are plenty of boring summer jobs out there. ∎

Wang Xiaofeng
Bart Simpson In Beijing

"CHINESE PEOPLE DON'T DO IRONY LIKE ISRAELIS AND THE English," says Wang Xiaofeng. "They don't have that making-fun-of-yourself gene." In China the blogosphere is indeed dominated by the dronings of millions of earnest diarists, and there are still many things that can't be said in the mainstream media. Wang, however, enjoys making fun of art, culture, politics—everything that Chinese people are supposed to hold dear. Serious critiques of social problems or political leaders can still be dangerous in China, but serious isn't Wang's style. He might be the most respected blogger in China, precisely because he respects almost nothing.

Wang's site gets about 12,000 visitors a day. It's plastered with pictures of the Simpsons—Wang is a fan of the show, and he likes to think he looks like Bart—but there's also a bit of Sacha Baron Cohen's slippery Borat character in Wang too. He has posted fabricated interviews and deliberately misleading surveys. Some people call him a cynic or a liberal; some people call him names that are shocking even by online standards of incivility.

But labels don't really fit Wang. He doesn't like isms and movements and refuses to join groups or parties. He doesn't have some big, catchall solution. "There's nothing that can be done about a lot of things in China," he says. "Most of what people do on the Internet is complain. At least we have a place to blow off some steam." ∎

ANAIS MARTANE FOR TIME

To read Wang's posts (in Chinese), go to *wangxiaofeng.net*

See Kamini's red-hot video at *kamini.fr*

DENIS ROUVRE FOR TIME

Kamini
Straight Outta Cowtown

KAMINI GREW UP IN A TINY town deep in the French countryside called Marly-Gomont. He stood out, in part because everybody stands out in Marly-Gomont—pop. 432—but partly because he's black. There aren't a lot of black people in Marly-Gomont.

Kamini (who keeps his last name private) wanted to be a hip-hop artist. So he recorded a song and shot a video with a friend. The total budget: 100 euros. In *Marly-Gomont*, Kamini raps about what he knows. "I couldn't rap about 'bitches' and 'hos' and do that whole gangsta thing," he says, "because it's not true. It's not my life."

Instead he raps about cows and tractors and soccer. "In Marly-Gomont," the song goes (it's in French), "there's no concrete/ 65 is the average age around here/ One tennis court, one basketball court." The video shows Kamini raisin' the roof with the village elders, who obviously think he's hilarious. But Kamini also raps about racism and being different: "I wanted to revolt, except that there, there's nothing to burn … Not worth going and burning a neighbor's car,/ Cuz they don't have them, they've all got mopeds."

On Aug. 30, Kamini and another friend put the video online and cold e-mailed some record companies to tell them about it. The response wasn't exactly a feeding frenzy. But an intern at one of the companies posted a link to the video on a bulletin board. "It's a site that sells custom-print T shirts," Kamini says, shaking his head. "It doesn't even have anything to do with music!" By the end of the day, nobody on the website was talking about T shirts. Everyone was talking about Kamini.

The video spread to YouTube and its French equivalents. Thousands of people watched it. Kamini started getting requests to appear on radio shows. In mid-October, without having toured or even played a single gig, he signed a record deal with RCA for *Marly-Gomont* and two albums. A rap star by popular proclamation, he had paid his dues virally. "Everything has happened in two months," says Kamini, who hasn't quit his part-time job as a nurse. "Look at me, sitting here at a luxury hotel being interviewed. How did all this happen?"

The answer is that the people can make their own stars now—no auditions, no promotions. It's like *American Idol,* but everywhere, all the time, although the bands that have broken through online—OK Go, the Arctic Monkeys, Lily Allen, Gnarls Barkley—are a lot more interesting than the bland standards belters on *American Idol.* Some rules haven't changed, it seems. People respond to talent and authentic emotion, and *Marly-Gomont* has both. ∎

THOMAS BROENING FOR TIME

Blake Ross
Outfoxing Microsoft

WHEN BLAKE ROSS WAS 15, HE MOVED FROM FLORIDA TO CALIfornia to take an internship with Netscape. This was a rather quixotic thing for a 15-year-old to do, because Netscape was on life support at the time—once it had ruled the WorldWide Web, but now its browser was getting the stuffing beat out of it by Microsoft's Internet Explorer.

Netscape had one thing going for it: it was open source. Most software is developed exactly the way you think it is: you pay a bunch of geeks in cubicles to write it. Open-source software works differently. You release a rough draft onto the Internet, and anybody can open the hood and go to work on it—streamline it, fix bugs, suggest features, pretty up the interface, whatever. In contrast, the people who write open-source software "aren't necessarily professionals," Ross says. "It gives you a breadth of experience outside of just computer geeks. It also means the people are truly dedicated because there's no payday." Open source is as much a community, even a subculture, as it is an approach to creating software.

In 2002 Ross and some colleagues decided to start up a new version of Netscape, one that would chuck all the fancy features and go for simplicity, stability and speed. They called the new browser Firefox, and it was a monster hit. When Firefox 2.0 appeared this October, it clocked 2 million downloads in the first 24 hours. Web surfers are switching to Firefox at the rate of 7 million a month.

There's something both very American and very anticapitalist about the open-source approach. It's about including everyone in the process, democratically, but it's also about giving away the product and sharing your trade secrets with the world; the more people who have a stake in your intellectual property the better. "I'm not in this for the money. I truly love it," Ross says. "I could never see myself sitting in a cubicle."

At the end of 2006, Ross, who is a world-weary 21, is taking time off from Stanford to work on a major new Web project whose code name is Parakey; top secret for now, it will be an open-source project. So Ross will make sure you hear about it.

—By Lev Grossman

Learn how you can join Ross's work at *blakeross.com*

YOUR WEB, YOUR WAY

IF THE WEB'S FIRST COMING WAS ALL ABOUT GRAFTING OLD businesses onto a new medium (pet food! on the Internet!), Web 2.0 is all about empowering individual consumers. It's not enough just to find that obscure old movie; now you can make your own film, distribute it worldwide and find out what people think almost instantly. Big businesses are embracing this new world as well, not just through advertising but also by tapping the expertise of everyone out there to enhance their products. Here's how to decode the buzzwords and blaze your own trail through the tangle of websites.

—By Jeff Howe

You Make It →→→→→→→

Web 2.0 is fueled by an outpouring of creativity from the people formerly known as consumers. From YouTube auteurs to bloggers to amateur photographers competing with the paparazzi, **USER-GENERATED CONTENT** is revolutionizing the media landscape

You Name It →→→→→→→→→→

The sheer mass of information online—20 billion Web pages and counting—should defy organization. Collective intelligence has risen to the challenge. With users tagging images, text and other forms of content, an organic sort of taxonomy has blossomed, appropriately called **FOLKSONOMY**

You Work on It →→→→→→→→→→→→→→→→→→→→

Why pay a professional when an amateur would do it for dramatically less money? In fields ranging from photography to the sciences, companies are taking jobs once performed by staff and **CROWDSOURCING** them to the enthusiastic, increasingly adept masses

You Find It →→→→→→→→→→

Wal-Mart can't afford to stock anything that won't sell in volume. But websites like MySpace or Netflix offer an endless array of obscure products, allowing users to forage successfully for Japanese ceramics or old-time bluegrass as easily as they might find the latest John Grisham book. This business model is known as the **LONG TAIL**

Jeff Howe is a contributing editor at Wired. *He writes about emerging trends at* crowdsourcing.com *and is currently working on a book about the crowdsourcing phenomenon*

THE ENTERTAINERS
The song remains the same, but the way we listen to it is changing. The movie, music, book and video-game industries have all embraced the Internet

BitTorrent
This efficient way of transmitting large files can make anyone a movie distributor

SECOND LiFE
An imaginary world built by users spending real money, it has become a nation of nearly 2 million

REVVER
By attaching ads to Web videos, Revver gave stupid pet tricks their first business model

You Tube
The site that leveled the entertainment playing field. *Ask a Ninja* outdraws *The Daily Show*

last·fm
the social music revolution
Beyond radio, it's a way to tap into the musical tastes of the crowd and add yours as well

NETFLIX
With more than 70,000 DVDs available, proof that Keanu and Kurosawa can coexist

iTunes
With a catalog of 3.5 million songs, Apple makes money off the misses as well as the hits

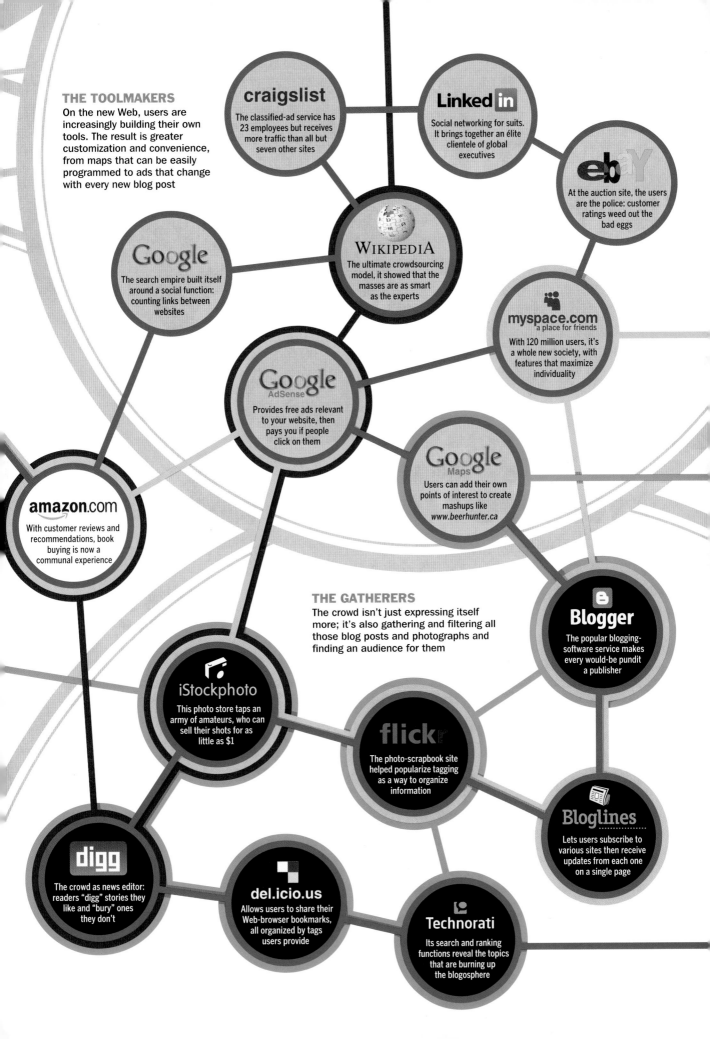

THE TOOLMAKERS
On the new Web, users are increasingly building their own tools. The result is greater customization and convenience, from maps that can be easily programmed to ads that change with every new blog post

craigslist
The classified-ad service has 23 employees but receives more traffic than all but seven other sites

Linked in
Social networking for suits. It brings together an élite clientele of global executives

ebaY
At the auction site, the users are the police: customer ratings weed out the bad eggs

Google
The search empire built itself around a social function: counting links between websites

WIKIPEDIA
The ultimate crowdsourcing model, it showed that the masses are as smart as the experts

myspace.com
a place for friends
With 120 million users, it's a whole new society, with features that maximize individuality

Google AdSense
Provides free ads relevant to your website, then pays you if people click on them

Google Maps
Users can add their own points of interest to create mashups like www.beerhunter.ca

amazon.com
With customer reviews and recommendations, book buying is now a communal experience

THE GATHERERS
The crowd isn't just expressing itself more; it's also gathering and filtering all those blog posts and photographs and finding an audience for them

Blogger
The popular blogging-software service makes every would-be pundit a publisher

iStockphoto
This photo store taps an army of amateurs, who can sell their shots for as little as $1

flickr
The photo-scrapbook site helped popularize tagging as a way to organize information

Bloglines
Lets users subscribe to various sites then receive updates from each one on a single page

digg
The crowd as news editor: readers "digg" stories they like and "bury" ones they don't

del.icio.us
Allows users to share their Web-browser bookmarks, all organized by tags users provide

Technorati
Its search and ranking functions reveal the topics that are burning up the blogosphere

THE YOUTUBE GURUS

How a couple of regular guys built an era-defining company that changed the way we see ourselves

L ET'S SAY YOU'RE IN YOUR 20S AND YOU START YOUR FIRST Internet company. Let's say 21 months later you sell it to search-engine giant Google for $1.65 billion. What happens next? At first, not much. Some of the money is tied up in escrow, and the traditions of modesty in Silicon Valley require a period of restraint before you spend in the big, life-changing way that your wealth will permit.

Still, the world wants to talk to you. Japanese television, Argentine newspapers, a bunch of French journalists and what seems like every news outlet in the U.S. Friends you haven't heard from in a long time send e-mails. *Hey, how's it going? Long time no see! BTW I have this great business idea …*

And so even though you've just left a photo shoot with an imperious, name-dropping L.A. photographer and driven to the airport in an Escalade, when you arrive at LAX, you have to stand in the United Economy line because you're still flying coach. When you walk past a newsstand, you see your company on the cover of *Wired* and *GQ*.

"Oh, and have you seen FORTUNE? … Yeah, we're in there too." And there they are: Steve Chen, 28, and Chad Hurley, 29, two of the three founders of YouTube (the other, Jawed Karim, went to grad school in 2005), a couple of boy-men looking out from a magazine and up at themselves in real life. Then they board the plane, Steve sitting way in the back and Chad closer to the front after paying an extra $24 for an "Economy Plus" seat.

Chad Hurley, Steve Chen and hundreds of the videos that helped turn YouTube into a sensation

movies—not even the main guy. Guys, you gotta know when to leave the party. *(When Leo does.)*

But of course the party is just starting for Chad and Steve, whose omnium-gatherum of online videos has captivated the Web for the past year, at least since a *Saturday Night Live* digital short called *Lazy Sunday* was forwarded millions of times last December, increasing visits to *youtube.com* by 83%. (If you don't know *Lazy Sunday*, don't tell anyone, particularly anyone under 30. Just quietly YouTube it now.)

YOUTUBE BECAME A PHENOMENON in 2006 for many reasons, but one in particular: it was both easy and edgy, a rare combination. You can watch videos on the site without downloading any software or even registering. YouTube is to video browsing what a Wal-Mart Supercenter is to shopping: everything is there, and all you have to do is walk in the door. Want to see Mikhail Baryshnikov performing in *Giselle* in 1977? A user named goldenidol uploaded a clip in August. Want to see a sure-to-make-you-queasy video of a girl snorting a strand of cooked spaghetti and then choking it out her mouth? You're in luck: asemoknyo put that clip on YouTube last month.

YouTube is a new kind of medium, but it's still mass. Your grandmother could use it (a search for "grandmother" on You-Tube yields more than 1,800 videos). But because the site doesn't prescreen uploads—which is a lot cheaper for Chad and Steve than hiring a bunch of editors to police millions of users—it ends up hosting a lot of out-there stuff as well: obscure bands, tear-jerking video diaries, "dead dog tricks" (don't ask), a "German toilet" (*please* don't ask) … The unmediated free-for-all encouraged the valuable notion that the site was grass-roots, community-run and—to use an overworked term—"viral." These are partial fictions, of course. YouTube controls the "Featured Videos" on its home page, which can dramatically popularize a posting that otherwise might fade. Also, the video in the top-right section of the home page is an advertisement, even though it doesn't always look like one. There's no porn on the site—overtly sexual material is flagged by users and removed by YouTube, usually very quickly. But there is an endless supply of kinda-weird, kinda-cool, kinda-inspiring stuff there, which means you can waste hours on Chad and Steve's site.

That, in turn, means advertisers want to be on YouTube, which is why Google paid so much for it. But for now, with YouTube still unproven—it has never made much money, and it could be crushed by lawsuits from content creators whose material shows up on the site without permission—the blockbuster acquisition price carries a whiff of the late-'90s Silicon Valley gold rush. It now falls to Chad, the CEO, and Steve, who runs the tech side, to prove that YouTube will not become the next *broadcast.com*, the video provider Yahoo! bought for $5.7 billion in 1999—and which now doesn't exist.

Turning YouTube from a sensational rumpus to a profitable corporation will require Chad and Steve to thread the company through legal disputes, hire at least 100% more employees than they have now, negotiate with the biggest ad and media companies in the world, maintain their unique identity without getting swallowed up by Google, please shareholders, manage p.r. and flawlessly execute a thousand other tasks that far more experienced executives have flubbed. All while Chad has to make time for his wife and two small children, Steve needs to buy a car to replace his crappy Jeep Wrangler, and the broadband in the YouTube office is so

Such is life these days for Chad and Steve—and because they are still young enough to get the occasional pimple, I don't mind calling them Chad and Steve. They are pre-moguls, near magnates. They foreshadow but don't quite yet embody the wealth and power that accompany their role as the new demiurges of the online world. At a *GQ* party in West Hollywood, Calif., a few weeks ago, Al Gore tapped Steve on the shoulder outside the bathroom to congratulate him on the success of YouTube. Chad chatted with Leonardo DiCaprio. But at the end of the night, the YouTube boys were hanging with the B crowd, Steve eating a burger (despite a disapproving glare from his girlfriend Julie) and Chad drinking until 2:30 a.m. with a guy who was in the *Jackass*

Karim is now a student at Stanford. He was friends with Chad and Steve at PayPal, but today his relationship with the other co-founders is somewhat strained

DOUGLAS ADESKO FOR TIME

PDA users to beam money to each other. Chad sent PayPal his résumé; the company flew him to California and asked him to show his skills by designing a company logo. His work is still in use, and he was hired as the company's first designer. He slept on a friend's floor for a few weeks, scrounging money for pizza before he got his first paycheck.

It was a propitious move; Chad had joined a firm that would soon abandon the handheld-payment concept in favor of something far more lucrative: securing online transactions. In 2002 eBay bought PayPal for $1.54 billion, and as an early employee, Chad walked away with enough to buy a few luxuries—including his Tag Heuer watch—and plenty of seed money for a future venture. Chad was also lucky to meet his future wife, Kathy Clark, at a party in 2000. Clark shared his interests in technology and in starting a family. She also turned out to be the daughter of James Clark, the legendary Silicon Valley entrepreneur who founded or co-founded three billion-dollar-plus companies: Silicon Graphics, Netscape and Healtheon. Chad insists, however, that Clark was not heavily involved in the creation of YouTube.

CHAD'S GREATEST STROKE OF LUCK at PayPal was meeting Chen and Jawed Karim, two PayPal engineers with whom he would occasionally bat around ideas for start-ups. Chen has always been something of a risk taker. The Taipei-born whiz kid left the University of Illinois at Urbana-Champaign a semester and a half early to work for PayPal, in part because several U. of I. alums worked there, including PayPal co-founder Max Levchin, who in turn was eager to hire Steve because of his educational background. Steve had attended not only U. of I.—which has a top-notch program in computer science—but also the Illinois Mathematics and Science Academy (IMSA), a widely respected state-funded boarding school.

Things always seem to work out for Steve, who carries an aura of mischief with him like a cloud of cigarette smoke. He drinks cappuccino well into the night and doesn't get to work until noon approaches. Levchin says that when Steve was an engineer at PayPal, he quickly established himself as the guy who could find the "shortest, cleverest path instead of hammering your head against the wall … He'd be, like, 'Yeah, I can get this feature done fast.'"

Karim, 27, enrolled at Stanford in 2005 to pursue a master's in computer science, and today there's some tension between him and the other founders, who have become famous while he toils in a small, modestly furnished dorm room. Although Karim is named on YouTube's site as a co-founder, Chad and Steve have promoted a highly simplified history of the company's founding that largely excludes him. In the stripped-down version—repeated in dozens of news accounts—Chad and Steve got the idea in the winter of 2005, after they had trouble sharing videos online that had been shot at a dinner party at Steve's San Francisco apartment. Karim says the dinner party never happened and that the seed idea of video sharing was his—although he is quick to say its realization in YouTube required "the equal efforts of all three of us."

Chad and Steve both say that the party did occur but that Karim wasn't there. No company, of course, is ever founded in a single moment, and YouTube evolved over several months. Chad and Steve agree that Karim deserves credit for the early idea that became, in Steve's words, "the original goal that we were working toward in the very beginning": a video version

slow that it takes forever to watch their own site. Can two kids who grew up nowhere near Silicon Valley handle all this?

CHAD MEREDITH HURLEY has the lanky and languorous carriage of a teenager who just rolled out of bed. He wears a stubble beard over a complexion that doesn't see enough sun, and he has a habit of pushing his chin-length hair back from his forehead so that by the end of the day it's a bit oily and Gordon Gekko–ish.

Raised in the southeastern Pennsylvania town of Birdsboro, he was an arty kid, always watercoloring and sculpting, which is not to say he ran with the artsy crowd. There is nothing affected or capering about Chad, and it's easy to imagine him as a slightly introverted, earnest boy trying to sell artwork (not lemonade) from his front lawn, as he did in an unsuccessful venture that taught him the difference between art and commerce.

Chad was unusual in that his artistic proclivities coincided with an interest in business and technology. In ninth grade, he built an amplifier that won third place in a national electronics competition. By the time he was in college, he would hole up for hours online, doing those things boys do these days—studying Web design, playing games, experimenting with animation. If it's true that people make their own luck, Chad made a lot of it. In 1999, he was finishing up at Indiana University of Pennsylvania, where he had majored in computer science before he switched to graphic design.

Around graduation, Chad read an article about a new company called PayPal, which back then was trying to enable of HOTorNOT.com, a dating site that invites viewers to rate, on a scale of 1 to 10, the attractiveness of potential mates. Karim says it was a pioneer: "I was incredibly impressed with HOTorNOT, because it was the first time that someone had designed a website where anyone could upload content that everyone else could view. That was a new concept because up until that point, it was always the people who owned the website who would provide the content."

As YouTube developed, Chad and Steve's complementary skills began to mesh. After Chad left PayPal in 2003, it seemed possible he would do something more artistic than be a CEO; he designed messenger bags, and he did a bit of work on a film Levchin helped fund, *Thank You for Smoking.* YouTube's success owes partly to its retro name, simple logo and alternative feel, all of which Chad contributed while Steve was making sure the videos played quickly and easily.

The idea of a video version of HOTorNOT lasted only a couple of months. "It was too narrow," says Chad. He notes that another early idea was to help people share videos for online auctions. But as the site went live in the spring of 2005, the founders realized that people were posting whatever videos they wanted. Many kids were linking to YouTube from their MySpace pages, and YouTube's growth piggybacked on MySpace's success. Indeed, MySpace remained YouTube's largest single source of U.S. viewer traffic in 2006, according to Hitwise.

Hurley, Chen and Karim, left, worked together at PayPal, whose logo Chad designed. Above, the three map out early YouTube concepts in Hurley's garage

YOUTUBE BY THE NUMBERS
Users upload 65,000 new videos to the site every day. A year ago, they watched 10 million videos a day; now they watch 100 million

Early on, Chad and Steve made a crucial good decision: despite pressure from advertisers, they would not force users to sit through ads before videos played. Pre-roll ads would have helped their bottom line in the struggling months, but the site would very likely never have gained its mythological community-driven status. It would have seemed simply like another Big Media site.

"In the end, we just sat back," says Chad—and the free-for-all began. Within months—even before *Lazy Sunday*—investors such as Time Warner and Sequoia Capital, a Menlo Park, Calif., investment firm, began to approach YouTube about buying in. Big advertisers started paying attention in October 2005, when a cool Nike ad-that-doesn't-look-like-an-ad of the Brazilian soccer player Ronaldinho went viral in

a big way on YouTube. Sequoia—which has helped finance Apple, Google and other valley greats—ended up providing about $8.5 million in 2005—just in time for Steve to avoid having to increase his credit-card limit yet again to pay for various tech expenses.

THE BIGGEST THREAT to YouTube's ongoing success remains potential copyright lawsuits from content providers that could claim that the site—like Napster before it—is enabling thieves. In a recent report, Google acknowledged that "adverse results in these lawsuits may include awards of substantial monetary damages." YouTube has responded by publicizing agreements it has made with media companies like NBC Universal Television to legally show video clips from, say, *The Office.* Still, YouTube says federal law requires only that it remove videos when copyright holders complain, as opposed to pre-emptively monitoring the site for infringements, which would destroy its spontaneity. If kids can't play sad pop songs in the background of their video blogs, why would they blog at all?

It's hard to imagine Chad and Steve sitting through endless meetings on safe-harbor laws. They're too young, too creative and—in Steve's case, at least—too peripatetic. But Levchin of PayPal says, "The essential crisis is coming. They better get ready. And the essential crisis for an entrepreneur is, What is this all about? Did I just make the most money in my life ever? For what purpose? And … am I going to start setting up my family office and manage my investments, or am I going to jump off another roof and hope there's a parachute?"

Which is a very old question indeed, one all newly wealthy people face when the market rewards them. Chad and Steve don't yet have an answer. They may have built a website that changed the online world in 2006, but they are still learning when to leave the party.

—By John Cloud

Society

Warning Signs

Motorists along Interstate 5 outside San Diego, Calif., are reminded to watch out for families of illegal aliens crossing into the U.S. from Mexico. Like a long-hidden disease that suddenly metastasizes, the simmering problems presented by America's growing population of illegal aliens finally burst into view in 2006. In Washington, the Senate and House of Representatives debated sharply different bills intended to stanch the flow of border-crossing illegals. In response, both legal and illegal immigrants and their suppporters marched through the streets in a host of U.S. cities, demanding amnesty for longtime residents with illegal status, declaring their devotion to their adopted country and emphasizing the important contribution they make to the nation's economy. Congress adjourned before a new bill was passed, leaving the highly emotional issue on the nation's front burner.

Warren Buffett

"Neither Susie [his late wife] nor I ever thought we should pass huge amounts of money along to our children." —Buffett

Billions of Reasons to Give

EARLY IN JULY, LEGENDARY INVESTOR WARREN BUFFETT strolled into a bank in downtown Omaha, Neb.,walked down a flight of stairs and inserted a key into his personal safe-deposit box. He pulled out a 27-year-old certificate for more than 120,000 shares of Berkshire Hathaway stock, which had been worth about $10 million when it was issued and had risen to a value of around $11 billion in the years since. Thus began the process by which the second richest man in the world began giving his fortune to the first. A few weeks earlier, Buffett announced he would donate most of his $40 billion bankroll to the Bill and Melinda Gates Foundation, which works to improve global health and U.S. education. The gift will come in a number of annual installments, with the proviso that each chunk of change must be spent in the year it's given. The $1.5 billion pledge for 2006 doubled the foundation's current spending and boosted its already powerful impact.

Buffett had long promised that his fortune would go to charity but had also insisted it would be handed off after his death. But this year he revised the timetable, coming up with a bold plan that raised the standards in philanthropy. The donations and pledges made by Buffett— and by Bill and Melinda Gates, who have given nearly $26 billion to their foundation so far—are without precedent, eclipsing by a wide margin the epochal gifts of earlier U.S. philanthropists. (Adjusted for inflation, the giving of titans Andrew Carnegie and John D. Rockefeller amounts to $7.2 billion and $7.1 billion, respectively.) The billionaire pledged to gradually give 85% of his Berkshire stock to five foundations. A dominant five-sixths of the shares will go to the Gates Foundation (the world's largest), the founders of which have been close friends of Buffett's since 1991, when they were introduced by a mutual friend. Buffett says he chose the Gates Foundation because, "they really have looked at the world without regard to gender, color, religion, geography. And they said, 'How can we do the most good for the most people and particularly the people that have gotten the short straws in life?'" ■

All His Trials

WHEN THE NEWLY CONVICTED FORMER CHAIR-man of bankrupt energy giant Enron died on July 5, Ken Lay left this world unrepentant, convinced he had done nothing wrong. Free on $5 million bond and awaiting sentencing after a Houston jury found him and former Enron CEO Jeffrey Skilling guilty in May on multiple counts of fraud and conspiracy, Lay continued to insist he was the victim of a vendetta by prosecutors and the media.

The year began inauspiciously for Lay and Skilling, when Enron's former chief accountant, Richard Causey, pleaded guilty to securities fraud in January and agreed to testify against his former bosses. That, along with the cooperation of Andrew Fastow, the company's onetime CFO (who pleaded guilty in 2004) was enough to seal the fate of both men. Fastow was sentenced to six years in August, as part of a plea agreement; Causey has agreed to serve between five and seven years, depending on the value prosecutors assign to his cooperation. Skilling was sentenced to 24 years and four months in prison. More than a dozen other former top Enron executives have pleaded guilty, been convicted in separate trials or are still awaiting trial for having inflated profits and hiding billions of dollars in debt while enriching themselves.

In October, a federal judge vacated Lay's conviction, agreeing with his lawyers' argument that a defendant who dies before exhausting all appeals has not had his full day in court. The ruling put Uncle Sam at the back of the line of claimants vying for $43 million in illicit profits from Lay's estate. ∎

Kenneth Lay

"Humility is a critically important trait in leaders ... There is no humility in either Skilling or Lay."
—Enron whistle-blower Sherron Watkins

Katie Couric

"Although it may be terrifying to get out of your comfort zone, it's also very exciting to start a new chapter in your life." —Couric

A Morning Percolator Becomes an Evening Anchor

THE CBS NETWORK, ACCORDING TO *TIME* ARTS CRITIC AND TV blogger James Poniewozik, is the Tevye of TV's Big Three networks, emphasizing "Tradition, tradition!" But the CBS News division turned its back on six decades of tube tradition in April 2006 when it hired NBC's longtime *Today* show anchor Katie Couric, 49, to replace Bob Schieffer as the anchor of its evening newscast. When she helmed her debut show on Sept. 5, Couric became the first woman to serve as the sole anchor of an evening news broadcast, the most prestigious job in TV journalism.

When Couric took over NBC's *Today* show in 1991, the show was in a ratings dive. Yet by the time she agreed to take the seat once held by Walter Cronkite and Dan Rather, *Today* had been the No. 1 morning show for more than a decade, and its success was attributed largely to Couric's infectious, try-anything attitude. Personable but persistent, Couric has a gymnast's flexibility and a sometimes deceptive amiability: more than one of her a.m. interviewees has fallen into the Venus flytrap of her neighborly charm. But her morning-show hosting duties included all sorts of nonsense, as *Today's* 3-hr. farewell show for Couric on May 31 proved: viewers again watched Katie flying through the air dressed as Peter Pan, Katie ice skating with Michelle Kwan, Katie kissing a chimpanzee. Some critics wondered whether Couric had the ballast to anchor a newscast. But considering how its audience has dwindled—fallen to competing media, changing schedules, apathy—the evening news may need less an anchor than a spotlight: someone who can get viewers' attention as well as their empathy.

Like Cronkite—albeit with a different style—Couric does both. On *Today* she created a bond with the audience that was part familial, part professional, as when she lost husband Jay Monahan to colon cancer, then drew on her experience for a series of reports on cancer awareness that landed her on the cover of TIME in 2000. Couric's star power alone generated a strong tune-in for her debut week on CBS; after that, an expected ratings slide followed. Couric will need to draw on her talent for mass intimacy to meet her ultimate challenge: to keep viewers interested in the news even after she has stopped being the news. ■

Shattering the Stained-Glass Ceiling

FOR YEARS NOW, AMERICA'S EPISCOPALIANS AND BRITAIN'S Anglicans have managed to paper over their deepening divisions by cooking up "Anglican fudge," makeshift measures that preserve an outward show of harmony. But the recipe seems increasingly unstable, and it may have not survive the latest U.S. ingredient: the election of Katharine Jefferts Schori as Presiding Bishop of the Episcopalian Church USA. Schori's selection in June at the U.S. church's general convention in Columbus, Ohio, came exactly 30 years after the historic Episcopal convention that made it possible, when the U.S. introduced the ordination of female priests. Schori's election to an office that puts her on a par with the worldwide Anglican Communion's 37 other national primates (including, technically, the religion's leader, the Archbishop of Canterbury) conclusively shatters what was once an Episcopalian "stained-glass ceiling." Of course, many of those other 37 primates refuse to elevate women to be bishops in their own countries.

The global Communion remains deeply divided on the subject of gays in the clergy. Schori voted for the election of American V. Gene Robinson, an active gay man, as a Bishop in 2003, although she did not attend his consecration. The Communion has demanded that the U.S. church "repent" Robinson's election. Schori, 52, who was the Bishop of Nevada before her election, is well equipped to calm the troubled waters: she's a former oceanographer. When TIME asked her about the condemnation by Communion conservatives of the U.S. church's liberal policies, she replied, "These decisions were made because we believe that's where the Gospel has been calling us." That doesn't sound like someone looking to make fudge. ∎

Bishop Katharine J. Schori

"The centrality of our mission is to love each other. That means caring for our neighbors. And it does not mean bickering about fine points of doctrine." —Schori

Immigration: America's

Passions are stirred but no legislation is passed as Congress tackles a swelling problem—the nation's reliance on millions of illegal aliens

F OR NEARLY AS LONG AS THE U.S. HAS BEEN A COUNTRY, THE question of who gets to be an American has excited our emotions and challenged our values as few others have. In 1886, the same year that the Statue of Liberty was dedicated in New York Harbor to the ideal of taking in the tired, the poor and the huddled masses yearning to breathe

free, racist mobs rioted in Seattle and forced more than half the city's 350 Chinese onto a ship bound for San Francisco.

More than 100 years later, the question of immigration continues to divide Americans. The two chambers of Congress, although directed by the same political party, considered two vastly different bills in 2006 designed to overhaul

New Dividing Line

the nation's immigration policy. Yet the fact that lawmakers were hotly debating major legislation to address the issue showed there is one thing about which everyone could agree when it comes to the current system: it's broken.

That message was evident far from the staid halls of Congress. It was shouted in a variety of languages by millions of voices on America's streets. The spark that lit the fuse was a bill introduced by Wisconsin Republican F. James Sensenbrenner in the House, which passed it in December 2005. The proposed new law called for the Federal Government to build two layers of reinforced fence along much of the 2,000-mile border with Mexico and declare everyone a felon who is illegally on the U.S. side of it—including an estimated 6 million undocumented immigrants from Mexico.

As the implications of the bill started to sink in, protesters began pouring into the streets of cities from Los Angeles to Philadelphia to vent their outrage. Suddenly, as if summoned from off-stage, the principals in the drama—illegal aliens and their American-citizen children—emerged from behind their shield of invisibility to demand citizenship. Their ranks included legions of voters who count the newcomers as family, friends and neighbors. Stunned by the size of the marches, Arizona Senator John McCain, who has long taken an interest in a subject very important to his constituents, said, "I never could have predicted that we would have 20,000 people in Arizona or half to three-quarters of a million in Los Angeles."

WALLS: Left, a barrier protects the U.S. border on a California beach. Above, Mexicans living in America rally in Los Angeles in April to protest a House bill that would make them felons

But the demonstrators were also sparking other reactions, especially after they ignored the pleas of rally organizers to wave only American flags. There was the scene in Apache Junction, Ariz., in which a few Hispanic students raised a Mexican flag over their high school and another group took it down and burned it. In Houston the principal at Reagan High School was reprimanded for raising a Mexican flag below the U.S. and Texas ones, in solidarity with his largely Hispanic student body. Tom Tancredo, the Colorado Republican who is Congress's loudest anti-immigrant voice, said his offices in Colorado and Washington were swamped by more than 1,000 phone calls, nearly all from people furious about the protests and the demonstrators "blatantly stating their illegal presence in the country and waving Mexican flags."

Mississippi Senator Trent Lott, describing the marchers, used language usually applied to the tantrums of children: "When they act out like that, they lose me." Virgil Goode, a Republican Congressman from Virginia, said, "If you are here illegally and you want to fly the Mexican flag, go to Mexico."

It has been 20 years now since the U.S. last overhauled its immigration policy. The measures approved in 1986 were intended to fix the root problem of an uncontrolled influx by making it illegal for U.S. employers to hire undocumented workers and offering an amnesty to illegal immigrants who had been here for five years at that point. Instead, the best estimates suggest that since then, the number of illegal immigrants has more than tripled. Local governments are staggering under the costs of dealing with the inflow. And since 9/11, controlling who comes into the country has become a security issue as well.

A TIME poll conducted in March 2006 suggested broad support for a policy makeover. Of those surveyed, 82% said they believe the government is not doing enough to keep illegal immigrants out of the country, and a large majority (75%) would deny them such government services as health care and food stamps. Half said children who are here illegally shouldn't be allowed to attend public schools. But only 1 in 4 would support making it a felony to be in the U.S. illegally, as the House voted to do when it approved the tough enforcement bill in 2005. Rather than expel illegal immigrants from the country, more than 75% of those polled favored allowing citizenship for those who are already here, if they have a job, demonstrate proficiency in English and pay taxes.

Social conservatives in the House who supported the 2005 bill argued that illegal immigration has begun an uncontrolled demographic and cultural transformation of the country, threatening its core values. Their primary concern was to protect the border and draw clear lines identifying illegal aliens as felons. In May 2006 the Senate passed a very different immigration bill, backed by G.O.P. Senators McCain and Pennsylvania's Arlen Specter and Massachusetts Democrat Edward Kennedy. It was designed to make citizens—and therefore voters—of millions of mostly Hispanic residents. The debate uncovered the deep divisions within the G.O.P. over the issue: while House Republicans feared the cultural impact of increased immigration, Senate Republicans heard from the business interests in the party base that fear a disruption of the steady supply of cheap labor for the agriculture, construction, hotel and restaurant industries, among others. It is their burgeoning demand for inexpensive labor

NABBED: At left, the hands of two Mexican men apprehended in California after crossing the border illegally are bound by U.S. agents. Above, illegal Mexicans wait at a California border crossing; they will be deported back to Mexico and released

that keeps illegal immigrants flowing into the U.S. and results in a shadow economy.

As House and Senate conferees tried to reach a compromise on the two different bills, the White House kept a close eye on the rift within the party, which threatened G.O.P. unity in an election year. Immigration policy was one of the ways in which George W. Bush defined himself in his 2000 campaign as a different kind of Republican, a Texas Governor who believed that "family values don't stop at the Rio Grande." Once in the White House, he infuriated some social conservatives by proposing an immigration plan that included a guest-worker program. It was an idea he shelved after 9/11, then put forward again as the first policy initiative of his 2004 re-election campaign. But in a private White House meeting with congressional leaders in 2005, Bush confessed

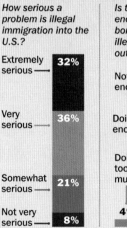
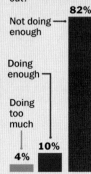

TIME POLL

LET THEM STAY, BUT GET TOUGH

While a majority of Americans want to crack down on illegal immigration, they also strongly favor guest-worker programs and temporary visas

How serious a problem is illegal immigration into the U.S.?	
Extremely serious	32%
Very serious	36%
Somewhat serious	21%
Not very serious	8%

Is the U.S. doing enough along its borders to keep illegal immigrants out?	
Not doing enough	82%
Doing enough	10%
Doing too much	4%

> ## "We want them coming in in an orderly way. And if they want to become a citizen, they can get in line, but not the head of the line."
> —George W. Bush, on his message to Mexican President Vicente Fox

that he had misjudged the politics of the issue and agreed to recalibrate, putting more emphasis on border security.

The President insisted, though, that he wants reform that includes both enhanced border enforcement and provisions for guest workers. Yet his ideas, which focus on giving migrant laborers temporary visas, have never gone as far as the McCain-Kennedy proposal of offering citizenship to illegal immigrants and some future guest workers. Bush is keen to preserve for Republicans the gains he is credited with having made among culturally conservative but traditionally Democratic Hispanics, who gave him 40% of their vote in 2004 and are believed to have been crucial to his re-election.

Early in the year, the time seemed right for a major overhaul of U.S. immigration policy, not least because the G.O.P.-controlled houses of Congress needed to prove they could work together to pass major legislation before the November elections. Yet despite the huge rallies in the nation's streets, despite the heated words in Congress and on the nation's editorial pages, despite a March meeting between Bush and Mexico's President, Vicente Fox, House and Senate Republicans found themselves too far apart on the issue to achieve anything approaching a compromise. In September Congress punted, handing the problem to the new legislatures that will convene in January 2007. *¡Adios, amigos!* ■

NO WORK! The large rallies protesting proposed immigration legislation took place across the nation and over a period of months. Above, a rally fills Wilshire Boulevard in Los Angeles on May 1, 2006, a day designated for a national boycott intended to show the importance of illegal aliens to the U.S. economy

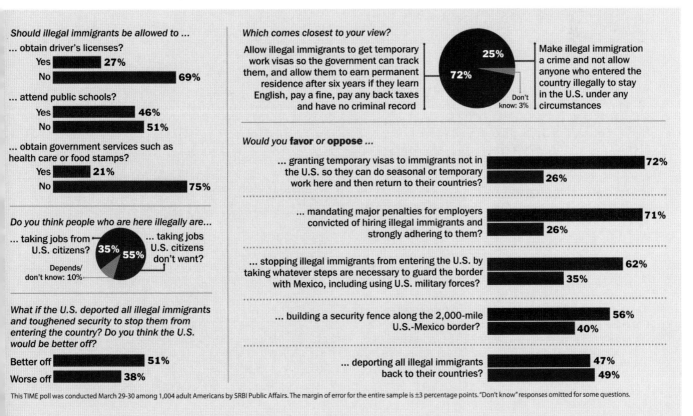

Should illegal immigrants be allowed to ...

... obtain driver's licenses?
Yes 27%
No 69%

... attend public schools?
Yes 46%
No 51%

... obtain government services such as health care or food stamps?
Yes 21%
No 75%

Do you think people who are here illegally are...
... taking jobs from U.S. citizens? 35%
... taking jobs U.S. citizens don't want? 55%
Depends/don't know: 10%

What if the U.S. deported all illegal immigrants and toughened security to stop them from entering the country? Do you think the U.S. would be better off?
Better off 51%
Worse off 38%

Which comes closest to your view?
Allow illegal immigrants to get temporary work visas so the government can track them, and allow them to earn permanent residence after six years if they learn English, pay a fine, pay any back taxes and have no criminal record — 72%
Make illegal immigration a crime and not allow anyone who entered the country illegally to stay in the U.S. under any circumstances — 25%
Don't know: 3%

*Would you **favor** or **oppose** ...*

... granting temporary visas to immigrants not in the U.S. so they can do seasonal or temporary work here and then return to their countries?
72%
26%

... mandating major penalties for employers convicted of hiring illegal immigrants and strongly adhering to them?
71%
26%

... stopping illegal immigrants from entering the U.S. by taking whatever steps are necessary to guard the border with Mexico, including using U.S. military forces?
62%
35%

... building a security fence along the 2,000-mile U.S.-Mexico border?
56%
40%

... deporting all illegal immigrants back to their countries?
47%
49%

This TIME poll was conducted March 29-30 among 1,004 adult Americans by SRBI Public Affairs. The margin of error for the entire sample is ±3 percentage points. "Don't know" responses omitted for some questions.

Tabloid Tempests

Brangelina and TomKat make babies, aging musicial outlaws make waves, and Mel Gibson makes a big mistake: the year in celebrity

If the Book Is Hissed, You Must Desist

Probing new depths in bottom feeding, HarperCollins editor-provocateur Judith Regan announced in the fall that she would publish *If I Did It,* a book in which O.J. Simpson would recount how he might have gone about murdering his ex-wife Nicole Brown Simpson and her friend Ronald Goldman in 1994. Simpson was found not guilty of the double murder in a controversial 1995 criminal trial but was found liable for the murders in a 1997 civil trial. The book, which was to be launched in tandem with a Fox TV interview with Simpson on Nov. 30, met with a firestorm of criticism. After weathering days of appeals to kill the project, media tycoon Rupert Murdoch, owner of Fox and HarperCollins, declared both the book and interview would be scrapped.

VINCE BUCCI—POOL—AP/WIDE WORLD

CHRIS POLK—AP/WIDE WORLD

Lindsay Lohan

The perennial party girl and former Disney teen queen, 20, faces the tough task of growing up in the public eye; two car accidents in 2005 made news. Morgan Creek Productions executive James G. Robinson gave her a scolding in a July letter, assailing her for the "all-night heavy partying" that he said slowed the filming of the upcoming *Georgia Rule.*

It's Better to Burn Out Than to Fade Away

It wasn't exactly a surprise when country-music outlaw Willie Nelson had a run-in with the law in 2006 over his possession of illegal substances. But Keith Richards, the bad-boy guitarist of the Rolling Stones for some 43 years, topped Nelson by having *his* run-in with a palm tree.

Nelson, now 73, has never denied his fondness for marijuana; country star Toby Keith's 2003 album *Shock'n Y'all* features a duet between the two, *Weed with Willie,* that recounts their adventures in inhaling on Nelson's biodiesel tour bus. Perhaps alert law officers heard the song: on Sept. 18, Nelson's bus was pulled over by Louisiana state troopers, who found 1.5 lbs. of marijuana and a stash of psychoactive mushrooms onboard. Busted!

Richards, 62, was vacationing on the island of Fiji on April 28 when he reportedly climbed a palm tree to fetch a coconut but fell down and broke his crown. Other reports had him falling off a jet ski; choose one. After minor brain surgery to relieve a blood clot, Keith rejoined his mates on their wildly successful Bigger Bang tour, clearly having outbanged his fellow Stones.

FROM LEFT: ROBERT E. KLEIN—AP/WIDE WORLD; PAUL MILLER—AP/WIDE WORLD

Exclusive!

First Baby Pictures!

Brad and Angelina welcome daughter Shiloh

The family in Namibia
June 3, 2006

Madonna's New Boy Toy

In her increasingly desperate attempts to avoid the public eye, chanteuse Madonna, 48, who first graced TIME's cover wearing her "boy toy" attire back in 1985, resorted to a new tactic in the live performances of her 2006 Confessions tour: a so-called disco crucifixion in which the entertainer belted out the song *Live to Tell* while mounted on a high-tech crucifix. A few priests objected: success! The tour supported her new album *Confessions on a Dance Floor,* which critics hailed as a strong return to form and reached No.1 on the pop charts in 41 countries. The 60-date tour reportedly grossed some $195 million.

Madonna, so often a trendsetter, was late in catching up to Hollywood's 2006 adopt-an-African-orphan craze. On a trip to Malawi in October, the star and British husband Guy Ritchie adopted a 13-month-old boy but were accused of having received special, accelerated treatment. Don't they know she's Madonna?

Stars: If You Think They're Just Like Us, You've Been Reading Too Many Tabloids

Flashing baby pictures was a major theme of the year in celebrity, as stars Angelina Jolie and Katie Holmes both welcomed daughters, giving new dads Brad Pitt and Tom Cruise more reasons to crow, if any were needed. (Another celebrity theme of the year: portmanteau marital names, as in the headline-friendly Brangelina and TomKat.) After the rituals attending star births ended—the sale of picture rights of the baby to magazines, with proceeds going to charity—Shiloh and Suri are bound to live happily ever after. In other nuptial news, music's Kid Rock tied the knot with flame Pamela Anderson on a yacht in the Mediterranean; the marriage lasted four months. Meanwhile Cruise's ex, actor Nicole Kidman, married country crooner Keith Urban, who entered rehab in October to fight a substance-abuse problem.

Mel, as in Meltdown

Talk about a road warrior: on July 28, at 2:36 a.m., one of Hollywood's biggest stars, Mel Gibson, was arrested on suspicion of driving on a Malibu highway under the influence of alcohol. The tip-off: Gibson, 50, was driving 87 m.p.h. in a 45-m.p.h. zone. Tests later revealed the actor's blood-alcohol content was 0.12%, well over the legal limit of 0.08%. But the arrest was only the beginning of his troubles. The man who became a hero to the Christian right for directing the 2004 monster hit *The Passion of the Christ* grew belligerent with police and flew into an anti-Semitic tirade, reportedly exclaiming, "The Jews are responsible for all the wars in the world," among other slurs. Upon reaching the police station, Gibson reportedly addressed a female police officer as "Sugar Tits" and had to be forcibly restrained. The popular actor subsequently issued several apologies for his behavior. On Aug. 17, Gibson pleaded no contest to one count of driving while intoxicated; he was sentenced to three years of probation, $1,600 in fines and will participate for a year in a 12-step program for alcoholism.

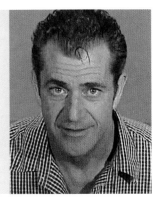

SocietyNotes

The Pope vs. Islam

Pope Benedict XVI, formerly Joseph Cardinal Ratzinger, sailed through his first year in the papacy—until Sept. 12, when he aroused the wrath of the Muslim world with his remarks at an academic conference at the University of Regensburg in his native Germany, shown here. In an erudite speech, the former academic quoted a 14th century Byzantine Emperor who said the Prophet Muhammad had brought "things only evil and inhuman" to the world. Benedict also questioned the concept of jihad, saying the idea of a holy war was unacceptable. His words sparked an uproar: Roman Catholic churches were burned, and an Italian nun in Somalia was killed. The Pope hastily apologized, but Muslim leaders continued to denounce the remarks. On a visit to Turkey in November, the Pope tried to mend fences, visiting a mosque and dropping his opposition to largely Muslim Turkey's admission to the European Union.

Alabama's Burning Issue

Three college students in Birmingham, Ala., were arrested on March 9 and charged with arson in a string of church fires. Ten fires were set in Alabama churches in the month of February; the three young men—Ben Moseley and Russell DeBusk, both 19, and Matthew Lee Cloyd, 20—were charging with setting nine of them. No one was injured in the fires, and race did not seem to be a factor. The youths told police that the crimes began as a joke, then got out of hand.

Judas Redeemed?

Capitalizing on the success of Dan Brown's *The Da Vinci Code,* the National Geographic Society backed the April publication of what it called a 2nd century Gnostic text, *The Gospel of Judas.* The fragmentary manuscript, whose provenance is not well documented, claims that Judas was complicit in Jesus' plans to die and was thus a hero rather than a villain. Both Anglican and Roman Catholic church leaders strongly questioned its authority.

Is There a Future for Ford?

When fourth-generation automaker Bill Ford appeared on TIME's cover in January 2006, he said his goal was to "restore a sense of confidence, externally and internally, in the company." But Ford's optimism was obsolete before the next model-year. On Sept. 5, the CEO and board chairman of the world's third largest automaker, above, announced he would hand his CEO duties to Boeing executive Alan Mulally.

Ford's new boss faces an army of barriers in turning the company around. In late October, Ford Motor announced it would lose $5.8 billion for the third quarter of 2006; its share price hovered around $8. Three of Ford's luxury brands, Aston Martin, Jaguar and Land Rover may be sold. Meanwhile, higher gas prices are killing two of Ford's strongest segments, pickup trucks and SUVs. And like GM, Ford pays crippling "legacy" costs for retiree benefits. Mulally said he would accelerate the company's previously announced Way Forward plan, which will add further cuts and closures to the 30,000 jobs and 14 factories already being eliminated. On Nov. 27, Ford said it had obtained $18 billion in financing for its recovery plan by mortgaging its assets for the first time in its history.

Mergers, Acquisitions and Other Big Deals

Big ... bigger ... biggest: U.S. companies continued to consolidate, merge and otherwise accumulate clout in 2006. A rundown of the top deals:

● **AT&T buys BellSouth** In the year's biggest deal, phone giant AT&T bought its rival and former Baby Bell, BellSouth, for $67 billion in March. AT&T was purchased in 2005 by SBC, which took over the famed name.

● **The Walt Disney Co. buys Pixar** For years, Disney created animated films the old-fashioned way: by drawing them. But beginning with Pixar's 1995 smash hit *Toy Story,* the industry moved strongly to computer-generated animation. Pixar's long string of hits, including *Monsters, Inc. Finding Nemo* and 2006's *Cars,* has been distributed in partnership with Disney. In January Disney announced it would acquire Pixar for $7 billion.

● **The McClatchy Co. buys Knight-Ridder** California-based McClatchy bought the 32 newspapers of the nation's second largest chain in June for $4 billion and quickly sold two of them, the Philadelphia *Inquirer* and San Jose *Mercury News.*

● **The WB merges with UPN** After vying for eyeballs and ad dollars since 1995, two weak cable-TV networks, CBS's UPN and Time Warner's WB, formed the new CW Television Network. It launched in September.

> **❝** The Lexus has been destroyed. We had it vaporized during yesterday's press conference. **❞**
>
> —**BILL FORD,** *referring to the top-of-the-line Toyota product previously driven by incoming Ford Motor Co. CEO Alan Mulally*

Hewlett-Packard's Boardroom Woes Continue

Hewlett-Packard, a pioneering Silicon Valley computer maker, has spent the past few years hopping between the frying pan and the fire. After charismatic CEO and board chairman Carly Fiorina was forced out of her position in 2005, Wells Fargo chief Patricia C. Dunn, right, took over. But on Sept. 22, Dunn resigned, following a boardroom scandal. Nearly two years ago, after the media started publishing things only an HP director could know, Dunn hired private investigator Ronald DeLia to find the leaker. His operation, which included PIs posing as journalists and HP directors to access their phone records, fell on the wrong side of the law, according to California's attorney general. On Oct. 4 the state filed criminal charges against Dunn and four others involved in the case.

A Former Racket Rebel Exits as a Beloved Elder Statesman

"I'm always changing," tennis ace Andre Agassi once said, and his journey from punk pariah to comeback champion to gracefully retiring elder proved his point. When first sighted in the late 1980s, Agassi was a long-haired teenager whose over-the-top court antics and in-your-face marketing persona made him seem more a cartoon than a contender. But after hitting an early peak, the wunderkind from Las Vegas suffered years of losses, including the deadliest loss of all: his belief in his talent. But Agassi kept reinventing himself: he shaved his head, tamed his demeanor and became one of only five men to achieve a career Grand Slam, winning Wimbledon and the Australian, French and U.S. Opens at least once. When, at 36, he contended for the last time as a pro, at the U.S. Open in September, he fought through severe back pain to thrill fans with a gallant victory over Greece's Marcos Baghdatis. That was Agassi's last hurrah—that, and the long round of affectionate cheers that ushered the onetime bad boy, now a grand old man of the game, into the tunnel following his loss in the next round to Germany's Benjamin Becker.

Sport

"I've basically grown up. When I look at myself 20 years ago, I understand that person a heck of a lot

more than I want to be that person." —Retiring tennis champion Andre Agassi

Roger Federer

"Roger just makes it look too easy. [He] puts fans in the position where all they can do is marvel." —Andre Agassi

The Cary Grant of the Baseline

WITH HIS 2006 VICTORY AT THE U.S. OPEN, ROGER FEDerer, 25, became the first player in tennis history to clinch both the British and U.S. singles titles for three consecutive years. Federer emphasized his current dominance of the men's game by also taking the 2006 Australian Open. The smooth Swiss has been the world's top-ranked player since 2004; only two other players, Ivan Lendl and Jimmy Connors, have held the title longer.

The unflappable, impeccable Federer is a study in tennis classicism. Who else would arrive at the Wimbledon final wearing a white sports jacket over his tennis duds? His game exudes a similar sense of high style: his volleys, awe-inspiring angled shots, and fluid one-handed backhand recall a bygone serve-and-volley era before today's high-tech racquets encouraged players to grip and rip missiles from the baseline. Says veteran tennis broadcaster Bud Collins: "He looks as though he woke up from a time capsule." Retired great John McEnroe agrees: "The way Roger moves, he's a ballet dancer out there. He floats above the court. His style is the most beautiful I've seen."

There's only one thing Federer needs at the moment: a great rival to challenge him. It was the fierce face-offs between McEnroe and Connors, and McEnroe and nerveless Swede Bjorn Borg, that drove the sport to its heights. Since 1992, the year Jimmy and Mac finally hung up their racquets, the number of Americans playing tennis has fallen 36%, to 11 million, according to the National Sporting Goods Association. Television ratings have trended south too. So fans everywhere who deeply admire Federer's game can be forgiven if they cheer for the colorful Spaniard Rafael Nadal or the gutsy American Andy Roddick to give Federer a run for his money. After all, the current king of the courts may just have been coasting till now: it would be thrilling to see this Swiss shift out of neutral. ■

Baseball's Big, Bad Redbird

ALBERT PUJOLS IS A DANGEROUS MAN. JUST ask any of the pitchers who have faced off with the St. Louis Cardinals 6-ft. 3-in first baseman. Pujols, 26, drilled home the message for the uninitiated in Game One of the 2006 World Series, when veteran Detroit Tigers manager Jim Leyland told Justin Verlander, the majors' best rookie pitcher of 2006, to try to strike Pujols out, rather than walk him. Good call: Verlander got three strikes past the right-handed hitter in the first inning. But when the superstar from the Dominican Republic came to bat again in the third, with a man on base, Verlander whizzed a 94-m.p.h. fastball down the pipe, and Pujols whacked it into the right-field seats of Detroit's Comerica Park. There was no joy in Motown, as the big blast ignited a 7-2 route. Even in Game Two, when the Tigers briefly revived the roar that had taken them from the worst record in the majors only three years ago to the 2006 Series, Pujols was the only Cardinal to earn a hit off of Detroit starter Kenny Rogers. That marked the Tigers' high point: Pujols, manager Tony La Russa & Co. returned to their new stadium in St. Louis and bagged, stuffed and mounted the Tigers, sweeping the last three games of the Series to win the Cards' first major league crown in 24 years.

For Pujols, 2006 was another routine year: he was on track to break Barry Bonds' single-season home-run record at the beginning of June but was sidelined for 15 games when he strained an oblique muscle. Yet he still racked up 49 homers and 137 RBIs and for a second consecutive year was the National League's Most Valuable Player. Here's Pujols on hitting: "I just try to see the ball," he explains, "and put a good swing on it." Thanks for the tip, Albert. That's inside baseball! ∎

Albert Pujols

"In my heart and mind, I know I can hit anybody. I'm always relaxed ... It's like playing with my kids. It feels natural." —Pujols

Dwyane's World

AFTER A STUNNING PERFORMANCE BY guard Dwyane Wade brought the Miami Heat their first ever NBA championship, fans and insiders alike began the inevitable litany of comparisons to Michael Jordan, Magic Johnson and Larry Bird. Like those all-time greats, the pro game's newest super-star is the antithesis of the all-too-familiar millionaire lout. Wade, 24, doesn't drink, sports no piercings or tattoos, and the closest he comes to locker-room cussin' is the occasional "bullcrap." When Wade was first recruited by the Heat after a promising career at Marquette University, he asked to wear No. 3, because it evoked the Holy Trinity. He even gives 10% of his multimillion-dollar salary to the church in the Chicago neighborhood where he grew up.

But where he really grew up, as far as fans are concerned, was in the 2006 NBA finals. After the Heat lost the first two games to the Dallas Mavericks, Wade rallied his team, scoring an average of 39 points in each off the next four outings. The consecutive victories swept the Heat to its first championship and transformed Wade from an emerging talent to a bona fide legend. Part of what makes Wade so unusual—and so valuable—is that he embodies the belief that a great player is less important than a player who makes the team great. Although he is remarkably versatile in his own right, the third-year pro's most striking talent is his natural leadership. Even vastly more experienced teammates like Shaquille O'Neal look to him for inspiration. This lofty status was ratified when Wade was named the championship tournament's Most Valuable Player.

Dwyane's World is an eclectic environment where both *Pride and Prejudice* (a favorite book) and Eminem lyrics reverberate. Lest he sound too perfect, the new king of the court does admit to a few vices, including a sadly deficient diet. "I'm a Quarter Pounder, double-cheeseburger, chicken-nuggets guy," he says. He skips Big Macs, however, explaining, "I'm not a vegetable eater." ∎

Dwyane Wade

"He's making his legacy in his third year. I mean, we are blessed to have him." —Miami Heat coach Pat Riley

Ben Roethlisberger

"If I ever ride again, it certainly will be with a helmet." —Roethlisberger, after his near fatal crash

How Big Ben Fell Down and Broke His Crown

OR PITTSBURGH STEELERS QUARTERBACK BEN ROETHLIS-berger, 2006 gave new meaning to the hackneyed coach's phrase, "a rebuilding year." After a stirring 21-10 victory on Feb. 5 over the Seattle Seahawks in Super Bowl XL made him, at age 23, the youngest NFL quarterback ever to win the championship, Roethlisberger planned to spend the off-season relaxing, resting his ailing knees and basking in the glory of having brought the fabled Pittsburgh team its first championship trophy in 26 years.

In June both Roethlisberger and his plans were upended when a motorcycle crash shattered his jaw, broke his nose, fractured his skull, gave him a concussion and caused so much bleeding that paramedics feared he might die (he was not wearing a helmet, per Pennsylvania law). After a surprisingly rapid recovery, the 6-ft. 5-in. quarterback, who is affectionately known as "Big Ben," went into training for the 2006-07 season and seemed to play even better in the preseason than he had the year before. Then, in the first week of September, just four days before the season-opening game against Miami, Roethlisberger awoke in the middle of the night with a bad stomachache. Within hours, he was rushed to a Pittsburgh hospital for an emergency appendectomy. It was his third surgery in 10 months; the knee problems that had sidelined him for three games in the 2005-06 season had also required an operation to fix.

Roethlisberger is a tough bird: he was back in the lineup by the second game of the season. But he was rusty, off his game: multiple interceptions and dropped balls cost the Steelers his first three games. Whether Roethlisberger can get the magic back remains to be seen. But either way, his brush with death made him a changed man. "What I learned," he reflects, "is it can end in a split second." ∎

Bravissimo, Torino!

Italy stages the 20th Winter Olympics, where a "Flying Tomato," skating dramas and snowboard traumas made for a glorious show in the snow

AMERICANS ARE FAMILIAR WITH TURIN, THE HISTORIC northern Italian city snuggled in the Alps that played host to the 2006 Winter Olympics, as the home of a mysterious shroud some believe once wrapped the body of Jesus Christ; it is also the home of the Fiat motor empire. But in 2006 we got to know a different city: Torino, a snazzy, upbeat, modern European metropolis. The capital of the Piedmont region worked hard to reinvent itself for the Games, building a new subway system and enlisting architect Renzo Piano to convert Fiat's onetime central auto factory, the Lingotto, into a spiffy cultural mecca that includes an art museum, a theater, a shopping mall and a five-star hotel.

The Winter Olympics are also trying to reinvent themselves, as officials continue to introduce the swagger and youthful appeal of X-game events like snowboarding and freestyle skiing into the familiar slate of cold-weather sports. The results can be jarring at times, as the intense focus of Alpine skiers or figure skaters runs up against the what-me-worry party spirit of the snowboard crew. When the breakout U.S. star of the Games, the shaggy halfpiper Shaun White, made a tele-

vised appeal for a date with the tightly wound figure skater Sasha Cohen, you had to hope he was blowing smoke.

White and his fellow medal-winning snowboarders, short-track speedskater Apolo Anton Ohno, Cohen and Alpine skier Ted Ligety were the biggest U.S. stars of the Games. Their medal harvest made up for the poor showing of the highly touted downhill skier Bode Miller, who seemed to have lost his inner fire just when he needed it most; he failed to medal. As for Canadian fans, they don't require stars; they simply believe it's their national birthright to win both the men's and women's hockey tournaments, and any other result won't do. So there was joy from Vancouver to Halifax when the women's team got the job done, but the seventh-place finish of the men's team left Canadians counting the days till 2010.

Olympic executives might be feeling the same way: U.S. TV ratings for the 2006 Games were down steeply from 2002, when Salt Lake City, Utah, was the venue. The reinvention of the Winter Olympics goes on—but for those who tuned in to Torino, the Games offered a colorful feast of sport that made good on their official slogan: Passion Lives Here. ∎

The Magic of the Metal

Gretchen Bleiler, left, and Hannah Teter, who took silver and gold in the women's halfpipe event, aren't hiding their medals under a bushel. The two U.S. athletes, who are good friends, dominated their event; indeed, the rest of the world is still struggling to catch up with the U.S. men and women in the showy halfpipe. Gold medalist Teter, only 19, is a member of a famed snowboarding family; Team Teter includes brothers Abe and Elijah. Bleiler, 25, took a year off after suffering a severe knee injury in 2003, but she regained her old form in time for Torino.

Boarder Cross? Boss!

Aiming to attract younger fans, Olympic officials continue to introduce new competitions to the Games. Among the most exciting of the batch that debuted in Torino was the snowboard cross event, which combines the newfangled thrills of 'boarding with the old-fashioned excitement of a foot race. With competitors swooping down the mountain, soaring over moguls, swerving over cambered turns and cutting off one another at hair-raising speeds, this was NASCAR on snow. American Seth Westcott and Swiss Tanja Frieden swooshed off with the first-ever gold medals in the event.

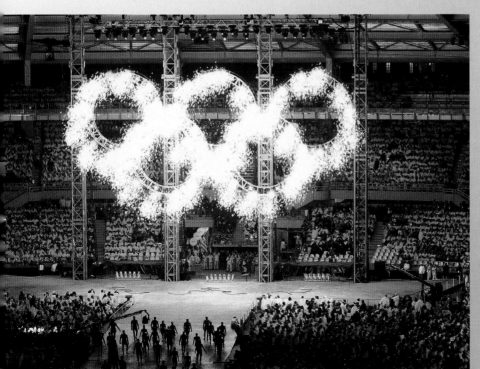

A Kitschy Kick-Off

For those hoping to re-create the opening ceremonies of the Torino Games in their backyards, the recipe list includes 122 makeup artists, 70 flame-thrower nozzles, 4,400 lbs. of fireworks and 6,500 costumes. And don't forget the fake cows pulled by Holsteinesque waltzers or the 28 white-clad acrobats who climbed poles to form an astonishing mid-air dove of peace.

Of course, your really big show won't be over until the fat man sings—and right on cue at Torino, Luciano Pavarotti appeared onstage and lifted his voice in *Nessun Dorma*. After that reminder of Italy's glorious cultural heritage, even your closing fireworks display may seem like an an anticlimax—as it did in Torino.

Bode in Free-Fall

In the winter of 2005, TIME reported that U.S. skier Bode Miller was by far the most popular competitor on the men's European skiing circuit. Indeed, the New Hampshire–born rebel's dashing style made him the most exciting U.S. downhill skier to appear in years. TIME put him on its cover before Torino, and hopes were high that the fiery 29-year-old would return from Torino with multiple medals. But something happened to Miller along the way: he was sour and sullen during the Games, and his usual party-boy antics seemed desperate rather than joyous. As for his skiing: well, this picture tells the story. Miller failed to medal.

A Rare Gold for U.S. Alpine Skiers

The Torino Games proved disappointing for U.S. skiers in the classic European Alpine events, particularly when the much ballyhooed Bode Miller flamed out in all his events. So it was up to Ted Ligety, left, to salvage Yankee pride, taking a surprising and very welcome gold medal in the Alpine Combined event. Ligety became the first American to triumph in an Alpine event since Tommy Moe won gold at the 1994 Lillehammer Games in Norway.

On Your Marks—Follow Apolo

In Torino, Apolo Anton Ohno, the sizzling short-track speedskater with the soul patch, repeated his dazzling performance from the 2002 Salt Lake City Games—although he couldn't repeat his earlier feat of becoming the youngest U.S. Olympic champion ever. Now a grizzled veteran of 24, Ohno took the gold medal in the shortest event, the 500 m. He also went home with bronze medals in the 1,000-m and 5,000-m relay events.

Sasha's Silver Lining

Television execs will tell you: for women viewers, the Olympic Games might as well be called the Figure-Skating Games. Hopes were high for a strong U.S. performance at Torino, with fast-rising Sasha Cohen hoping to give longtime favorite Michelle Kwan a run for the gold. But Kwan withdrew, and although Cohen skated well, she was edged out for first place by the elegant, if a bit reserved, skating of surprise winner Shizuka Arakawa of Japan, who became a national hero as Japan's first-ever gold winner in the event.

A Sibling Stand-In

What would women's figure skating be without a crisis or two? At Torino, Michelle Kwan set the stage for drama when she withdrew from the Games, leaving a vacancy on the U.S. team. Who you gonna call? Why, the younger sister of 2002 gold medalist Sarah Hughes, Emily. With TV tracking her movements by the minute, Hughes raced from New York City to Torino and put on a fine display of skating, long on spirit and poise if a tad shy on technique. The 17-year-old's star-making turn was a highlight of the Games.

Snowboard Showboat

U.S. athlete Lindsey Jacobellis earned a place right up there with Wrong Way Corrigan on sport's all-time boo-boo list with her performance in the women's snowboard cross event. Leading Tanja Frieden of Switzerland as she swooped off the penultimate hill, Jacobellis tried an airborne hot-dog maneuver that was pure show, grabbing her board in a move called a backside grab. But she landed on the edge of her board and fell, finishing second. She later said, "Snowboarding is fun. I was having fun." Frieden may have had even more fun.

JUGGERNAUT: The game's No. 1 player holds the Claret Jug awarded to the winner of the British Open, which he has now won three times. Woods proved again in 2006 that his only real competition is with the greatest players of the past

Par for the Course

Phil Mickelson once again proves he's a master of disaster, while Tiger Woods overcomes a personal tragedy and further burnishes his legend

F OR GOLF FANS, 2006 WAS A TALE OF TWO CHAMPIONS, PHIL Mickelson and Tiger Woods. And once again, like Charlie Brown and Lucy revisiting their familiar jerk-the-football routine, the game's two brightest stars obliged their fans by playing the roles seemingly assigned to them at birth. The emotional Mickelson, 36, won the year's first major event, the Masters Tournament, only to snatch defeat from the jaws of victory in the second, the U.S. Open. The icy Woods, 31, came on strong after a slow start to win the year's last two majors, the British Open and PGA Championship.

Fan favorite Mickelson was in fine form early at the Masters in Augusta, Ga. It was on this course in 2004 that "Lefty" broke through to win his first victory in the four major tournaments that have come to define greatness in golf. The famed course had been lengthened yet again to take into account today's long-hitting pro game—it is now some 7,445 yds.—and when rain hit the course on Saturday, the tournament turned into a punishing ordeal, as the game's best players rose to the top for Sunday's final round. Mickelson, who had trailed by four strokes going into the Saturday round, made a strong charge and won the right to wear the green jacket for a second time, beating South Africa's Tim Clark by two strokes; Woods finished tied for third.

A buoyant Mickelson rolled right into the U.S. Open at the

IN THE PINK: O.K., maybe their jackets are a bit, uh, whimsical for U.S. tastes, but the beaming Europeans wearing them handed yet another drubbing to the Yanks in Ryder Cup play

Winged Foot course in Westchester, N.Y., only to break fans' hearts with his historic collapse on the last hole (*see* Images), when he carded a double-bogey to hand the coveted trophy to Briton Geoff Ogilvy. Woods, however, had a miserable Open: his father Earl, the Vietnam veteran whom the champion has always credited as his greatest mentor and inspiration, lost a long battle with cancer shortly after the Masters, and Woods took nine weeks off the tour to mourn. At Winged Foot, Woods failed to make the field-narrowing cut after the second round for the first time in his professional career.

Yet golf fans have learned never to doubt Woods' mental toughness. He dominated the field at the year's third major, the British Open in the Royal Liverpool Golf Club. Using his driver only once on the seaside links course, he shot 18 strokes under par, beating American Chris DiMarco by two shots to win his third Claret Jug. After his final putt, the man who seems to be made of ice surprised a global TV audience by breaking into tears as he saluted his late father, whom he had earlier described as "an amazing dad, coach, mentor, soldier, husband and friend."

Back on track, Woods prevailed again at the PGA Championship at the Medinah Country Club outside Chicago, when he again finished at 18 under par. The victory put Woods' total number of major championships at 12, extending one of the most exciting ongoing stories in sports, as Tiger pursues his long-established goal of topping the 18 major trophies that adorn the mantel of his boyhood idol Jack Nicklaus.

But even Woods couldn't help his countrymen prevail at September's Ryder Cup in Kildare, Ireland. Although Woods won the majority of his matches, the Yanks were once again humiliated by the Europeans, who have now won five of the past six biennial events. Tiger's game may be out of the woods, but when it comes to Ryder play, the U.S. is still in the rough. ∎

TRIUMPH: Phil Mickelson won his second Masters trophy in April, here, but went down in flames in the U.S. Open in June

England's David Beckham

England's Wayne Rooney

Brazil's Ronaldo

Italy's triumph

Color Us Red, White And Very, Very Blue

At soccer's gaudy World Cup, the Americans just aren't on the ball

EVERY FOUR YEARS, U.S. SPORTS FANS ARE REMINDED OF the gulf that separates them from their counterparts around the world, thanks to soccer's World Cup. As nations from the Andes to Africa virtually shut down for the five summer weeks when Cup play dominates the news, many Yanks remain immune to the appeal of the world's most popular sport. That divide is also evident on the field of play, even though the U.S. team is now consistently winning entry to the 32-team tournament and managed a best ever run to the quarter-finals in 2002.

Yet hope springs eternal for American soccer fans, who point to the continuing growth of youth play as a harbinger of better years to come; it's been 10 years since "soccer moms" became shorthand for a political subgroup. And although the women's pro league, which was formed after the U.S. team won the World Cup in 1999, shut its doors in 2003, franchise owners in the men's U.S. pro circuit are busy building a new generation of fan-friendly stadiums.

Even so, when the teams assembled in Germany for the 18th global tournament, the U.S. squad, coached by veteran Bruce Arena and led by standouts Landon Donovan and Claudio Reyna, found itself outmatched by the world's best players; the U.S. did not advance to the "knockout round" of 16. The star-spangled teams that did advance provided plenty of highlights for fans to chew over: the strangely uninspired play of the popular Brazilians; England's frustrating quarter-final loss to a surprising Portugal squad; the host team's lifeless loss to Italy in the semifinals. And for fans in Togo, Angola, the Ivory Coast, Ukraine, the Czech Republic and Trinidad and Tobago, there was joy in their nation's simply taking part in the Cup for the first time.

The thrilling final pitted Italy's defense-minded *Azzuri* against a dashing French team that had won the Cup on home soil in 1998. Thanks to French midfielder Zenédine Zidane's vicious head-butt of Italy's Marco Materazzi in overtime, the game—and Italy's 5-3 victory on penalty kicks in overtime—will be long remembered, maybe even in Podunk. ∎

U.S.A.

Japan

Togo

Germany

Australia

Sweden

Mexico

Kobe Bryant

Two years after he was cleared of a rape charge in a criminal case in Colorado, Bryant, 27, apparently believes he has something left to prove. The Los Angeles Lakers' great shooting guard thrilled NBA fans on Jan. 22, when he scored 81 points against the Toronto Raptors, left. It was the second highest scoring effort by an individual in NBA history, after Hall of Famer Wilt Chamberlain's 100-pt. game in 1962. Bryant's last-second winning shot in Game 4 of the playoffs against the Phoenix Suns was another all-time stunner.

Floyd Landis

After watching Lance Armstrong win the Tour de France for seven years in a row, Americans hoped to see a fellow Yank ride through the streets of Paris wearing the yellow jersey of a champion. And Armstrong's onetime teammate, Floyd Landis, 31, seemed to get the job done. Yet less than a week after his apparent victory, race officials claimed Landis had tested positive for the presence of testosterone, a banned substance, in his urine; they later declared they no longer considered him the champion and would begin formal proceedings to strip him of the title.

Landis strongly maintains he is innocent; he is scheduled to present his formal appeal to retain his championship in 2007.

Heroes or Villains?

From cycling to sprinting to baseball, athletes are charged with abusing drugs to perform better. But they're also abusing fans—and their sports

SAY IT AIN'T SO, FLOYD! PERHAPS THE MOST TELLING SPORTS story of 2006 was the rapid rise and and even swifter fall of U.S. cyclist Floyd Landis. Few Americans had heard of the amiable Pennsylvania Mennonite before this year's Tour de France, but they began paying attention when Landis moved to the head of the pack. Yet just when victory seemed within reach, Landis fell back in the peloton, six minutes behind the leaders. But wait! Landis then moved back in the lead, thanks to a stirring uphill comeback in the Alps that was swiftly dubbed the Ride of the Century. Days later, Landis proudly wore the yellow jersey of the Tour winner underneath the Arc de Triomphe, the toast of his countrymen.

But the arc of Landis' narrative allowed precious little time for triumph. Within a week of his victory, the American rider was charged with doping. It may be that Landis is innocent; he has stoutly declared he is. But there's a larger innocence involved here that seems in increasing danger of being lost: the essential belief of the fan in sport as a world in which rules matter and superiority is earned, not injected. Doping is the enemy of sports. Say it ain't so, Floyd. ∎

Barry Bonds

Perhaps no athlete in 2006 was the target of so much vilification as Bonds, 42. The San Francisco Giants' slugger hit his 715th home run on May 28, left, passing Babe Ruth on the all-time homer list, and finished the season needing only 10 homers to tie Henry Aaron's lifetime record of 755. But many fans reviled Bonds, believing he was guilty of using steroids, in the past if not the present. A highly damaging 2006 book, *Game of Shadows*, by two respected San Francisco *Chronicle* writers, charged Bonds with extensive use of steroids, beginning in 1998. But the star has never been formally charged with misdeeds.

Asafa Powell

The grinning man at left is Asafa Powell, celebrating after matching his world-record time of 9.77 sec. in the 100-m dash in Zurich, Switzerland, on Aug. 18. Powell, 23, a Jamaican who still trains in his hometown of Kingston, dazzled the world of track in 2006 with a series of 100-m sprints that either matched or set new world records; he is the only man in history to have run three sub-9.8 100-m sprints. The Jamaican and his chief rival, America's Justin Gatlin, dueled throughout the year, pushing each other to personal bests. For months the two men shared the world record, but Gatlin's best time, set in April, was disallowed in August after he tested positive for using performance-enhancing drugs. He was banned from the sport for 8 years.

Marion Jones

The sprinter TIME heralded in 2000 as "the marvelous Marion Jones" has hit more than her share of rough patches in the past few years, including a disappointing 2004 Olympics and a divorce from husband C.J. Hunter. Jones weathered another crisis in 2006: in June she was accused of using the endurance booster erythropoietin, but a follow-up test cleared her. Jones, 30, said she was "ecstatic" to have avoided a possible two-year ban from racing.

SportNotes

Tragedy on the Track

There was no clear favorite in the 2006 Kentucky Derby, so when the previously undefeated Barbaro, the second choice of the betting public, roared into high gear and won the race by 6½ lengths, the Thoroughbred became the immediate favorite to win the second event in racing's Triple Crown, the Preakness Stakes. But in the Maryland classic, as the horses rounded the final turn, Barbaro suddenly reared up, with his right hind leg sticking out at an awful angle: he had shattered three bones and dislocated a joint in his foot. In earlier days, he would have been put down, but—amid a huge outpouring of public affection—Barbaro was taken into surgery at the University of Pennsylvania's George D. Widener Hospital for Large Animals, where his leg was reset in a 4-hr. operation. The surgery was chancy, yet against the odds, Barbaro survived and is thriving. The injury raised new questions about whether owners are pushing young horses too far, too fast.

More Drug Scandals Beset the Tour de France

A housewife enjoys a baguette and a sideline view of one of sport's most colorful events, the Tour de France, as cyclists roll from Beauvais to Caen in Stage 5 on July 6. Yes, the Tour is long on charm—but it also seems far too long on substance abuse. The 2006 event ended with apparent victor Floyd Landis accused of using forbidden testosterone. Yet it also began with a scandal, as 13 athletes were banned for doping only days before the race started, including renowned riders Jan Ullrich and Ivan Basso.

NASCAR's Reign of Kahne

The good people at NASCAR seem to treat their product, stock-car racing, with the same loving attention the sport's drivers give to their cars. By constantly tweaking and supercharging their races, stars and marketing programs, NASCAR's front-office grease monkeys have driven their sport to steadily increasing popularity. In 2006, only NFL football games outdrew NASCAR races in TV ratings.

One way NASCAR stays fresh: by producing exciting young drivers like Kasey Kahne. Only 26 and in his third full year on the Nextel Cup circuit, Kahne won six races in 2006 and qualified in 10th position for the season-ending Chase series of races, edging out the veteran fan favorite Tony Stewart. Born in Enumclaw, Wash., Kahne grew up a long way from Copenhagen Nation but has now made amends by settling down in North Carolina. He drives one of America's favorite muscle cars, a Dodge Charger.

Conquistador of the Clay

The exciting Spaniard Rafael Nadal, 20, is a perfect foil for the suave king of men's tennis, Roger Federer. The duo met in two big finals in 2006: Nadal showed his mastery of the clay court, beating the smooth Swiss to win the French Open in June, but Federer trounced Nadal at Wimbledon in July, and Nadal faded quickly at the U.S. Open in September. Wait till next year!

Grunting Her Way to Glory

Tennis fans have learned by now that watching Maria Sharapova play the game involves the ears as much as the eyes: each of her sizzling strokes seems to be powered by the mighty howl she emits as she whales the ball. But whatever her formula for success, it's working: in 2006 the 6-ft. 3-in. Russian, who has lived in the U.S. since age 7, kept improving her game. At left, she celebrates her victory over Belgian Justine Henin-Hardenne in the U.S. Open on Sept. 9. Still a teenager—she's only 19—Sharapova promises to become one of the game's all-time greats.

> **“** The scoreboard says I lost today, but what the scoreboard doesn't say is what I have found. And over the past 21 years, I have found loyalty … I've found inspiration … And I've found generosity. **”**
>
> —**ANDRE AGASSI,** *retiring from tennis after his final match at the U.S. Open*

Southern Discomfort at Duke

On March 14, a 27-year-old black woman told police in Durham, N.C., that she had been repeatedly raped by three members of the almost all-white lacrosse team at Duke University, one of the nation's premier colleges. The exotic dancer, a mother of two and a student at a mainly black college in Durham, had performed at a team party but fled the house, right, after her alleged rape.

The case pushed America's hot buttons, touching on divisions of race, gender and class, as well as the perception that college athletes are privileged brats, granted immunity from academic and social norms. The story made headlines for weeks, but as time passed, serious questions were raised concerning the accuracy of the woman's account. As of Nov. 1, 2006, the three athletes charged in the case were still awaiting trial.

Science

Oklahoma, Where the Fire Comes Sweepin' Down the Plain

For cattle ranchers and their herds along a broad swath of the wide-open spaces of the Southwest, from Kansas and Oklahoma to west Texas, the year 2006 arrived in the midst of a deadly string of wildfires, the result of a long dry spell that turned generally verdant pastures brown and brittle. These cattle are fleeing a Jan. 1 grass fire outside Guthrie, Okla., some 35 miles north of Oklahoma City, that was the final inferno in a series of such blazes that began in November 2005, spurred by months of drought and unrelenting heat. By the time the last flames in Oklahoma and Texas were put out, around Jan. 3 in most places, four people had died, some 331,000 acres of grassland had been scorched and more than 250 homes and buildings had burned to the ground. Ten days later, a new string of grass fires lit up the plains. Calling his state a "tinderbox," Texas Governor Rick Perry declared the entire Lone Star State a disaster area.

GERRY BROOME—AP/WIDE WORLD

"It's knocked a big hole in our livelihood." —Oklahoma rancher Gayla Stacy, 53

Hollywood's Green Avenger

AL GORE USED TO JOKE THAT IT WAS EASY TO pick him out in a roomful of Secret Service agents: he was the stiff one. So he would be the first to say how surreal it was to find himself the toast of the film world in the summer of 2006, when the lecture on global warming he had been giving for decades to any audience that would let him set up his flip charts was turned into the surprisingly successful documentary *An Inconvenient Truth.* The movie made the usual indie-film circuit, winning raves at Sundance and Cannes, but its real impact was felt in movie theaters in the U.S., where audiences across the political spectrum declared its study of the perils of global warming both compelling and convincing. Soon, TV wit Stephen Colbert was joking that Gore's movie was "the highest-grossing PowerPoint presentation in history."

In some ways, Gore's film followed a standard mutant-action-hero storyline: it was the tale of a political has-been transformed into a laptop-wielding ninja whose slide show could rescue the planet from the forces of greed and indifference. And like any blockbuster, the 92-min. documentary spawned a passel of spin-offs: a book with the same title; a website (*www.climatecrisis.net*); and a training program in Nashville, Tenn., that will enable 1,000 activists "to give my slide show in their voices," employing a limited-use license to remix the music and images. But the best measure of the film's impact may be the fact that it also inspired an ad campaign financed by the oil industry to discredit it.

Rather than retire to the sidelines of public life after the 2000 election, Gore has stayed in the game by continuing to fight for the environment and other causes close to his heart: as a teacher, as an investor whose fund puts its money in socially responsible ventures and as an entrepreneur who founded the youth-oriented television network, Current, launched in 2005. The former Vice President's renaissance has also prompted renewed speculation about whether he might bid for the White House again, possibly as soon as 2008. Or maybe that's just hot air. ■

Al Gore

"I can't imagine any circumstances in which I would become a candidate again ... I've found other ways to serve." —Gore

Absolute Monarch of the Valley of the Kings

ALTHOUGH HE IS MOST OFTEN PHOTOGRAPHED IN HIS trademark Indiana Jones fedora, Zahi Hawass wears many hats. The head of Egypt's Supreme Council of Antiquities sometimes plays the telegenic media darling; on other occasions he is cast as a controversial bureaucratic tyrant, the King of De Nile, ruling over who will excavate in Egypt—and who will not. But at all times, Hawass manages to dodge the single most pervasive occupational hazard that afflicts his colleagues in archaeology: he is never boring.

In February archaeologists announced the discovery of a new tomb in the Valley of the Kings, the first untouched find since Howard Carter entered King Tutankhamen's tomb in 1923. Inside the tomb (which Hawass, characteristically, would not permit to be opened until he had arrived at the site) were seven coffins. On the basis of several clues, such as pottery with inscriptions identical to some found with Tut, Hawass whipped up a storm of speculation that Tut's mother Queen Kiya might be inside one of them. When the casket was opened, Hawass had his Geraldo Rivera moment: Kiya was nowhere to be seen.

Undeflated, Hawass, 58, resumed his whirlwind schedule of lectures, TV appearances and book tours while also publishing a seemingly endless stream of articles. His predecessors mainly kept a low profile, but Hawass doesn't hesitate to use words like magical, thrilling and marvelous when describing discoveries in the area he has heavily promoted as the Valley of the Golden Mummies. Nor is he reluctant to accuse or offend: he makes news by demanding the return of objects "stolen" from Egypt by excavators and museums, such as the Rosetta Stone. (The charge is accurate in some cases, but not all.) His recent edicts restricting new excavation, particularly in such popular sites as Saqqara and the Valley of the Kings, have aroused the ire of some foreign archaeologists.

Hawass hopes his most lasting legacy will be his focus on conserving the antiquities. The irony of his career is that his greatest enemy may be himself: with his P.T. Barnum showman's swagger, he has helped encourage the very tourism, central to Egypt's economy, that threatens the historic monuments he protects. ■

Zahi Hawass

"Hawass [rules] with an iron fist and censorious tongue. Nobody crosses him and gets away with it." —Britain's *Sunday Times*

WILDFIRES: Out-of-control blazes in Indonesia, the Western U.S., above, and even inland Alaska have been increasing as timberlands and forest floors grow more parched. The fires pour more carbon into the atmosphere and reduce the number of trees, whose leaves help fight global warming by inhaling carbon dioxide and releasing oxygen

FLOODS: As warmer ocean waters help fuel larger and more devastating tropical storms, hurricanes and typhoons, major floods like the one that struck India in 2006, above, are becoming more common. One possible result of increasingly warm waters: tropical storms could begin turning up in places they have never struck before, such as Canada

The Year's Hottest Story

Once dismissed as overhyped conjecture, global warming is now widely accepted as a scientific reality and a very serious threat to life on Earth

N O ONE CAN SAY EXACTLY WHAT IT LOOKS LIKE WHEN A planet takes ill, but it probably looks a lot like Earth. Never mind what you've heard about global warming as a slow-motion emergency that would take decades to play out. Suddenly and unexpectedly, the crisis is upon us. It certainly looked that way in 2005 as curtains of fire and dust turned the skies of Indonesia orange, thanks to drought-fueled blazes sweeping the island nation. It certainly looked that way in March 2006 as the atmospheric bomb that was Cyclone Larry—a Category 5 storm with wind bursts that reached 185 m.p.h.—exploded through northeastern Australia. It certainly looks that way as sections of ice the size of small states continue to calve from the disintegrating Arctic and Antarctic ice shelves. And it certainly looks that way as

MELTING ICE CAPS: Too much carbon dioxide in Earth's atmosphere traps solar heat, melting polar ice. A 2005 study found that the Greenland ice cap is melting more than twice as fast as it did as recently as in 1996. One result: polar bears, like this pair traveling across melting ice floes in the Arctic, may not survive the century

TOP: EVELYN HOCKSTEIN—POLARIS. BOTTOM: ARCTICNET—NCE

the sodden wreckage of New Orleans continues to molder. Disasters have always been with us and surely always will be. But when they hit this hard and come this fast—when the emergency becomes commonplace—something has gone grievously wrong. That something is global warming.

The image of Earth as organism—famously dubbed Gaia by environmentalist James Lovelock—has probably been overworked, but that's not to say the planet can't behave like a living thing, and these days, it's a living thing fighting a fever. From heat waves to storms to floods to fires to massive glacial melts, the global climate seems to be crashing around us. Scientists have been calling this shot for decades. And that is precisely what they have been warning would happen if we continued pumping greenhouse gases into the atmosphere, trapping the heat that flows in from the sun and raising glob-

al temperatures. Environmentalists and lawmakers spent years shouting at one another about whether the grim forecasts were true, but in the past five years or so, the serious debate has quietly ended. Global warming, even most skeptics have concluded, is the real deal, and human activity has been causing it. If there was any consolation, it was that the glacial pace of change in the planet's natural systems would give us decades or even centuries to sort out the problem.

But glaciers, it turns out, can move with surprising speed, and so can nature. What few people reckoned on was that global climate systems are booby-trapped with tipping points and feedback loops, thresholds past which the slow creep of environmental decay gives way to sudden and self-perpetuating collapse. Pump enough CO_2 into the sky, and that last part per million of greenhouse gas behaves like the 212th degree Fahrenheit that turns a pot of hot water into a plume of billowing steam. Melt enough Greenland ice, and you reach the point at which you're not simply dripping meltwater into the sea but dumping whole glaciers. By one recent measure, several Greenland ice sheets have doubled their rate of slide, and in March 2006 the journal Science published a study suggesting that by the end of the century, the world could be locked in to an eventual rise in sea levels of as much as 20 ft. Nature, it seems, has finally got a bellyful of us.

"Things are happening a lot faster than anyone predicted," says Bill Chameides, chief scientist for the advocacy group Environmental Defense and a former professor of atmospheric chemistry. "The last 12 months have been alarming." Says Ruth Curry of the Woods Hole Oceanographic Institution in Massachusetts: "The ripple through the scientific community is palpable."

And it's not just scientists who are taking notice. Even as nature crosses its tipping points, the public seems to have reached its own. For years, popular skepticism about climatological science stood in the way of addressing the problem, but the naysayers—many of whom were on the payroll of energy companies—have become an increasingly marginalized breed. In a 2006 TIME/ABC News/Stanford University poll, 85% of respondents agree that global warming probably is happening. Moreover, most respondents say they want some action taken. Of those polled, 87% believe the government should either encourage or require lowering of power-plant emissions, and 85% think something should be done to get cars to use less gasoline. Even Evangelical Christians, who formerly took no position on environmental issues, are demanding action, most notably in February 2006, when 86 Christian leaders formed the Evangelical Climate Initiative, demanding that Congress regulate greenhouse gases.

Such public stirrings are at last getting the attention of politicians and business leaders, who may not always respond to science but have a keen nose for where votes and profits lie. State and local lawmakers have started taking action to curb emissions, and major corporations are doing the same. Wal-Mart has begun installing wind turbines on its stores to generate electricity and is talking about putting solar reflectors over its parking lots. HSBC, the world's second largest bank, has pledged to neutralize its carbon output by investing in wind farms and other green projects. Even President George W. Bush, hardly a favorite of green activists, now acknowledges climate change and boasts of the steps he is taking to fight it. Most of those steps, however, involve re-

VICIOUS CYCLES

The debate over whether Earth is warming up is over. Now we're learning that climate disruptions feed off one another in accelerating spirals of destruction. Scientists fear we may be approaching the point of no return

TIME graphic by Joe Lertola; reported by Missy Adams

THE GREENHOUSE EFFECT

Without the **greenhouse effect,** life on Earth would not be possible. Energy from the sun is absorbed by the planet and radiated back out as heat. Atmospheric gases like **carbon dioxide** trap that heat and keep it from leaking into space. That's what keeps us warm at night.

But as humans pour ever increasing amounts of greenhouse gases into the atmosphere, more of the sun's **heat gets trapped,** and the planet gets a fever

SUNLIGHT

HEAT

How Hot Will It Get?
Global annual average temperatures and projections

Actual temperatures

56.79°F (13.77°C)

57.97°F (14.43°C)

approx. **66°F (19°C)**

Range of temperature projections

approx. **61.5°F (16°C)**

Celsius / Fahrenheit

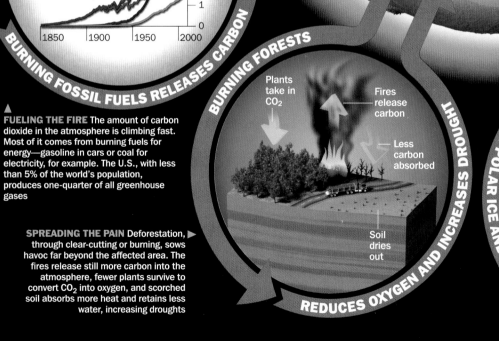

Global CO$_2$ emissions, in billions of metric tons

- Total from fossil fuels
- From liquid-fuel consumption
- From solid-fuel consumption
- From gas-fuel consumption

BURNING FOSSIL FUELS RELEASES CARBON

FUELING THE FIRE The amount of carbon dioxide in the atmosphere is climbing fast. Most of it comes from burning fuels for energy—gasoline in cars or coal for electricity, for example. The U.S., with less than 5% of the world's population, produces one-quarter of all greenhouse gases

SPREADING THE PAIN Deforestation, ▶ through clear-cutting or burning, sows havoc far beyond the affected area. The fires release still more carbon into the atmosphere, fewer plants survive to convert CO$_2$ into oxygen, and scorched soil absorbs more heat and retains less water, increasing droughts

BURNING FORESTS

Plants take in CO$_2$

Fires release carbon

Less carbon absorbed

Soil dries out

REDUCES OXYGEN AND INCREASES DROUGHT

MELT POLAR ICE AND PERMAFROST

RISING

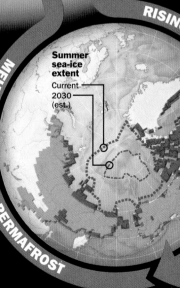

Summer sea-ice extent

Current
2030 (est.)

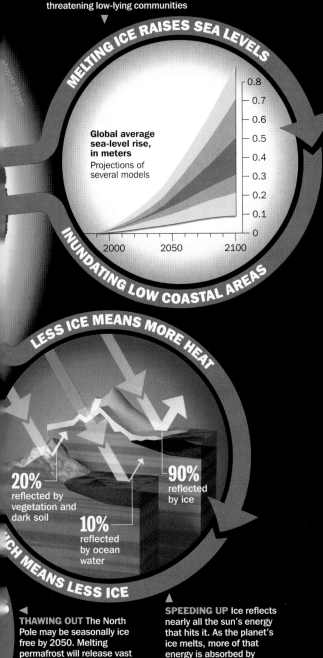

WASHING ASHORE The ice at the North Pole is floating, so as it melts, the sea level won't change much. But the massive ice sheets over Antarctica and Greenland are another story. If both melted completely, sea levels could rise nearly 220 ft. (72 m). That's a worst-case scenario. But the melting is accelerating, and sea levels are projected to rise gradually, threatening low-lying communities

MELTING ICE RAISES SEA LEVELS

Global average sea-level rise, in meters
Projections of several models

INUNDATING LOW COASTAL AREAS

LESS ICE MEANS MORE HEAT

20% reflected by vegetation and dark soil

10% reflected by ocean water

90% reflected by ice

'CH MEANS LESS ICE

THAWING OUT The North Pole may be seasonally ice free by 2050. Melting permafrost will release vast amounts of trapped carbon into the air

Near-surface permafrost
■ 1980-99
■ 2080-99 (est.)

SPEEDING UP Ice reflects nearly all the sun's energy that hits it. As the planet's ice melts, more of that energy is absorbed by Earth—which further raises the temperature. That, in turn, makes the remaining ice melt quicker

Sources: Intergovernmental Panel on Climate Change, Third Assessment Report; NOAA; NASA; National Snow and Ice Data Center; Carbon Dioxide Information Analysis Center; National Center for Atmospheric Research; U.S. Global Change Research Program; Goddard Institute for Space Studies

search and voluntary emissions controls, not exactly the kind of federal action scientists are calling for: laws with teeth.

Is it too late to reverse the changes global warming has wrought? That's still not clear. Reducing our emissions output year to year is hard enough. Getting it low enough so that the atmosphere can heal is a multigenerational commitment.

It is fitting, perhaps, that as the species causing all the problems, humans have experienced the effects of global warming in terrible ways. Ocean waters have warmed by a full degree Fahrenheit since 1970, and warmer water is like rocket fuel for tropical storms. Two 2005 studies found that in the past 35 years the number of Category 4 and 5 hurricanes worldwide has doubled while the wind speed and duration of all hurricanes has jumped 50%. Scientists suspect tropical storms could start turning up in some unusual places. "There's a school of thought that sea surface temperatures are warming up toward Canada," says Greg Holland, senior scientist for National Center for Atmospheric Research in Boulder. "If so, you're likely to get tropical cyclones there ... we honestly don't know."

So much environmental collapse happening in so many places at once has at last awakened much of the world, particularly the 141 nations that have ratified the 1997 Kyoto treaty to reduce emissions—an imperfect accord, to be sure, but an accord all the same. The U.S., however, which is home to less than 5% of Earth's population but produces 25% of CO_2 emissions, remains intransigent. President Bush's rhetorical nods to America's oil addiction and his praise of such alternative fuel sources as switchgrass early in 2006 have yet to be followed by real initiatives.

The U.S. Congress has not been much more encouraging. So, increasingly, state and local governments are filling the void. The mayors of more than 200 cities have signed the U.S. Mayors Climate Protection Agreement, pledging, among other things, that they will meet the Kyoto goal of reducing greenhouse-gas emissions in their cities to 1990 levels by 2012. Nine Eastern states have established the Regional Greenhouse Gas Initiative for the purpose of developing a cap-and-trade program that would set ceilings on industrial emissions and allow companies that overperform to sell pollution credits to those that underperform—the same smart, incentive-based strategy that got sulfur dioxide under control and reduced acid rain. And California passed the nation's toughest automobile-emissions law in the summer of 2005.

"There are a whole series of things that demonstrate that people want to act and want their government to act," says Fred Krupp, president of Environmental Defense. Krupp and others believe that CO_2 concentrations will keep climbing higher but can be stabilized and then dialed back down.

Curbing global warming may be an order of magnitude harder than, say, eradicating smallpox or putting a man on the moon. But is it moral not to make the effort? We did not so much march toward the environmental precipice as drunkenly reel there, snapping at the scientific scolds who told us we had a problem. The scolds, however, knew what they were talking about. In a solar system crowded with sister worlds that either emerged stillborn like Mercury and Venus or died in infancy like Mars, we're finally coming to appreciate the knife-blade margins within which life can thrive. For more than a century we've been monkeying with those margins. It's long past time we set them right. ■

Earth to Pluto: Get Lost

After international astronomers vote to downgrade the outermost planet from the sun, a host of Plutophiles raises an outcry: Poor little Pluto!

WHEN THE WORLD'S PROFESSIONAL STARGAZERS ASsemble to discuss celestial matters—well, it's over most people's heads. But the 2006 gathering of the International Astronomical Union (IAU) in Prague brought cosmic concerns right down to Earth—or, more precisely, right into the classrooms and bedrooms of children around the world, whose decorations often include mobiles showing the nine planets orbiting the sun. In the days after the astronomers voted to downsize the outermost planet in the solar system, reclassifiying Pluto as a "dwarf planet," parents and teachers everywhere were faced with the pleas of weeping kids, outraged on Pluto's behalf. For stargazing tykes, it was the biggest news in the heavens since the cow jumped over the moon.

Yet for those who follow astronomy, the news came as no surprise. Pluto has always been an outsider among the planets. To begin with, it's tiny: at 1,600 miles in diameter, it is even smaller than Earth's moon. And its elongated orbit is off-kilter, at a steep angle to the ecliptic, compared with those of the other planets. At times during its 248-year revolution of the sun, Pluto moves inside Neptune's orbit.

Even the familiar story of Pluto's discovery raised questions. The object was found in 1930 by the American astronomer Clyde W. Tombaugh during a systematic search for a trans-Neptunian Planet X, predicted by Percival Lowell and William H. Pickering. In a series of photographs he had taken at the Lowell Observatory in Flagstaff, Ariz., Tombaugh recognized the new planet by its motion, which was slower than that of numerous asteroids also recorded on the same photographs. At the time Tombaugh was only 24 and a relative amateur in the field of astronomy; the story of his painstaking research has been used by teachers for decades as a classroom parable about the importance of disciplined study and the opportunity for even amateurs to contribute to our knowledge of the heavens. But in fact, the distortions supposedly driven by the gravity of Planet X never actually existed; they were the result of imprecise measurements.

When the Rose Center for Earth and Space opened at New York City's Museum of Natural History in 2000, Pluto was not included among the eight large models of the planets of the solar system revolving around the sun that were a centerpiece of the new hall. The resulting outcry over the museum's unilateral downgrade was one reason for the 2006 re-evaluation of Pluto's status.

When the astronomers assembled in Prague this summer, they were originally presented with an expanded, rather than diminished, model of the solar system. This early proposal would have increased the number of planets in the solar system to 12, retaining Pluto's status as a planet and adding several of the large trans-Neptunian objects that have been

Largest Known Kuiper Belt Objects

"Gabrielle"

Charon

"Xena"
(2003 UB313)

Pluto

2005 FY9

2003 EL61

Sedna

Quaoar

Under the new, 2006 definition of solar system objects, Pluto is no longer a planet but rather a dwarf planet located in the Kuiper Belt, the immense disc of relatively small objects beyond the orbit of Neptune and thus described as trans-Neptunian objects (TNOs). The Kuiper Belt, named for Dutch-American astronomer Gerard Kuiper, is the source of most comets that orbit the sun. In recent years, astronomers have discovered a number of new large TNOs, including "Xena" (now Eris), Sedna, Quaoar and two as-yet-unnamed bodies. Pluto's moon Charon was discovered in 1978.

discovered in recent years in the Kuiper Belt *(see sidebar)*.

But the astronomers later voted to reject this save-Pluto scheme and approved a new definition of what constitutes a planet. Under this new terminology, a planet is defined by three main critieria: it must orbit the sun, it must be big enough for gravity to have squashed it into a round ball, and it must have cleared other celestial objects out of its orbital path. The final criterion was the trigger for Pluto's downgrade; it also applies to the larger objects in the Kuiper Belt, as well as to Ceres, the largest object in the asteroid belt between Mars and Jupiter.

On his informal blog *Eye on Science* at TIME.com, the magazine's longtime science writer Michael Lemonick called the astronomers' decision a good one for four reasons. First, it righted the historical error caused by the mistake over the supposed distortions caused by Planet X. Second, we now know that there are thousands of objects in the far reaches of the solar system, some nearly as big as Pluto and at least one that's bigger—and, like Pluto but unlike the planets, they're

MEET ERIS: This artist's conception shows Kuiper Belt object 2003 UB313. The body was nicknamed Xena by its discoverer, Michael Brown of the California Insitute of Technoloy (who called its moon, just below, Gabrielle). Larger than Pluto, Xena was renamed Eris shortly after the 2006 IAU conference; Gabrielle is now Dysnomia

all made mostly of ice. Pluto is a very large member of a class of objects that aren't like planets. So calling it a planet isn't really a scientifically useful way to categorize it.

Lemonick's third point directly addressed the wailing schoolkids and their elders. "The point of teaching science," he wrote, "as some people too easily forget, is not to create happiness but to explain how the world works and how we know. This change provides a valuable teaching moment. When a child asks, 'Why did they pick on poor Pluto?' the answer will tell them something new we've learned about the universe and how we learned it. Science is about discovery, not about memorizing lists of things."

Lemonick's fourth point: the vigorous debate in Prague proves that science is a human enterprise that includes passion and politics. The first proposed definition of a planet, which included Pluto and the three other objects, was soundly rejected by the delegates, who demanded something more scientifically valid. Another teaching moment: scientists don't always agree.

On the other hand, Lemonick could point out only one reason why the decision was a bad one: we can no longer use the mnemonic "My Very Energetic Mother Just Served Us Nine Pizzas" to remember the planets in order from the sun. His solution: Change "Nine Pizzas" to "Nachos." Another cosmic problem solved.

Or not: the issue of Pluto's identity may persist. The vote to downgrade Pluto was taken in the final moments of the astronomers' meeting and was approved by fewer than 500 of the more than 2,000 astronomers in attendance. Planetary scientist Alan Stern of the Southwest Research Institute and a few other skeptics soon circulated a petition among fellow skywatchers that stated, "We, as planetary scientists and astronomers, do not agree with the IAU's definition of a planet, nor will we use it. A better definition is needed." Within days, the petition boasted 300 signatures, including a number from some very prominent scientists at very prominent institutions. In other words, hang onto the model of Pluto that fits on your mobile for now—and hold the nachos. ∎

Stem Cells:
The Promises and the Protests

As science and politics collide over medicine's exciting new frontier, TIME explores the complex research and realities behind the heated headlines

CELLULAR: A blastocyst, above, consists of a very small number of cells. Opposite page: a University of Wisconsin technician works with embryonic stem cells, which grow rapidly under certain conditions

WHEN THERE'S NOTHING ELSE TO PRESCRIBE, HOPE works like a drug. A quadriplegic patient tells herself it's not a matter of if they find a cure but when. Who's to say whether salvation is still 10 or 15 years away? After all, researchers have been injecting stem cells into paralyzed rats and watching their spinal cords mend. "Stem cells have already cured paralysis in animals," declared Christopher Reeve in a commercial he filmed a week before he died.

But what is the correct dose of hope when the diseases are dreadful and the prospects of cure distant? When President George W. Bush in July vetoed the bill that would have expanded funding for human embryonic-stem-cell (ESC) research, doctors got calls from patients with Parkinson's disease saying they weren't sure they could hang on for another year or two. The doctors could only reply that even in the best-case scenario, cures are at least a decade away, that hope is no substitute for evidence and that stem-cell science is still in its infancy.

It is the nature of science to mix hope with hedging. It is the nature of politics to overpromise and mop up later. But the politics of stem-cell science is different. Opponents of ESC research argue that you can't destroy life in order to save it; supporters argue that an eight-cell embryo doesn't count as a human life in the first place—not when compared with the life it could help save. Opponents say the promise of embryo research has been oversold, and they point to the cures that have been derived from adult stem cells from bone marrow and umbilical cords. Supporters retort that adult stem cells are still of limited use, and to fully realize their potential we would need to know more about how they operate—which we can learn only from studying leftover fertility-clinic embryos that would otherwise be destroyed.

Back and forth it goes, the politics driving the science, the science pushing back. Stem-cell research has joined global warming and evolution science as fields in which the very facts are put to a vote, a public spectacle in which data wrestle dogma. Scientists who are having surprising success with adult stem cells find their progress being used by activists to argue that embryo research is not just immoral but also unnecessary. But to those in the field, the only answer is to press ahead on all fronts. "There are camps for adult stem cells and embryonic stem cells," says Douglas Melton, a co-director of the Harvard Stem Cell Institute. "But these camps only exist in the political arena. There is no disagreement among scientists over the need to aggressively pursue both in order to solve important medical problems."

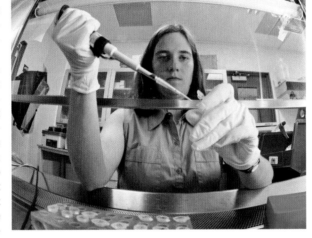

Stem-cell research has joined global warming and evolution science as fields in which the very facts are put to a vote, a public spectacle in which data wrestle dogma

Trapped in all this are patients and voters who struggle to weigh the arguments, for the science is dense and the values tangled. Somewhere between the flat-earthers who would gladly stop progress and the swashbucklers who disdain limits are people who approve of stem-cell research in general but get uneasy as science approaches ethical frontiers. Adult-stem-cell research is morally fine but clinically limiting, since only embryonic cells possess the power to replicate indefinitely and grow into any of more than 200 types of tissue.

Extracting knowledge from embryos that would otherwise be wasted is one thing, but scientists admit that moving forward would require a much larger supply of fresh, healthy embryos than fertility clinics could ever provide. And once you start asking people about creating embryos in order to experiment on them, the support starts to slow.

So where do things stand, five years after Bush provided the first federal funding but radically limited how it could be used?

In a prime-time speech from his Texas ranch in August 2001, Bush announced that federal money could go to researchers working on ESC lines that scientists had already developed but that no new lines could be created using federal funds. "There is at least one bright line," he declared. The speech was a political and scientific landmark. It gave Democrats that rare gift: a wedge issue that split Republicans and united Democrats, who quickly declared themselves the party of progress. Five years later, with midterm-election races in progress, Democrats hoped to leverage the issue as evidence that they represent the reality-based community, running against the theocrats. States from Connecticut to California have tried to step in with enough funding to keep the labs going and slow the exodus of U.S. talent to countries like Singapore, Britain and Taiwan.

Meanwhile, private biotech firms and research universities with other sources of funding are free to create and destroy as many embryos as they like, because they operate outside the regulations that follow public funds.

For scientists who choose to work with the approved "presidential" lines, the funding comes wrapped in frustration. Today there are only 21 viable lines, which limits genetic diversity. They are old, so they don't grow very well, and were cultured using methods that are outdated. The presidential lines, scientists say, are wasting money as well as time. Congress tried to address the problem with a bill to allow funding for research on any leftover embryos donated by infertility patients. But even if Bush hadn't vetoed that bill, it wouldn't have solved the supply problems. One study estimated that at best, a couple hundred cell lines might be derived from leftover IVF embryos, which tend to be weaker than those implanted in patients. The very fact that they come from infertile couples may mean they are not typical, and the process of freezing and thawing is hard on delicate cells.

In the wake of Bush's original order, Harvard University decided to use private funding to develop about 100 new cell lines from fertility-clinic embryos, which it shares with researchers around the world. Scientists, desperate for variety, snap them up. At the same time, Harvard has opened another battleground in the search for cells. After exhaustive ethical review, its researchers announced in the summer of 2006 that they would develop new cell lines through somatic cell nuclear transfer, or therapeutic cloning. In this process, a cell from a patient with diabetes, for instance, is inserted into an unfertilized egg whose nucleus has been removed; then it is prodded into growing in a petri dish for a few days until its stem cells can be harvested. Unlike fertility-clinic embryos, these cells would match the patient's DNA, so the body would be less likely to reject a transplant derived from them.

Even more exciting for researchers, however, is that this technique can yield embryos that serve as the perfect disease in a dish, revealing how an illness unfolds from the very first hours. The long-term promise is boundless, but the immediate barriers are high. The only people who claim to have succeeded in creating human-stem-cell lines through nuclear transfer were the South Korean researchers whose work turned out to be fraudulent. It will take much trial and error to master the process, but where do you get the human eggs needed for each attempt, particularly since researchers find it ethically inappropriate to reimburse donors for anything but expenses? And even if the technique for cloning embryos could be perfected, would Congress allow it to go on?

To get around political roadblocks, scientists are searching for another source of cells that is less ethically troublesome, ideally one that involves no embryo destruction at all. One approach is "altered nuclear transfer," in which a gene, known as CDX2, would be removed before the cell is fused with the egg. That would ensure that the embryo lives only long enough to produce stem cells and then dies. That strategy, promoted by Dr. William Hurlbut, a member of the President's Council on Bioethics, has its critics. Dr. Robert Lanza of biotech firm Advanced Cell Technology considers it unethical to deliberately create a crippled human embryo "not for a scientific or medical reason but purely to address a religious issue." The most exciting new possibility doesn't get near embryos at all. Dr. Shinya Yamanaka of Kyoto University reported tantalizing success in taking an adult skin cell, exposing it to four growth factors in a petri dish and transforming it into an embryo-like entity that could produce stem cells—potentially sidestepping the entire debate over means and ends.

Even if scientists discover an ideal source of healthy cell lines, there is still much to learn about how to coax them into turning into the desired kind of tissue. Parkinson's patients suffering from tremors caused by damaged nerves could benefit from replacement neurons, while diabetics who can't produce insulin could control their blood sugar with new pancreatic islet cells. But so far, researchers have not been

WHAT THEY ARE

Stem cells are nature's master cells, capable of generating every one of the many different cells that make up the body. They have the ability to self-renew, which means that they are theoretically immortal and can continue to divide forever if provided with enough nutrients. Because they are so plastic, they hold enormous promise as the basis for new treatments and even cures for disorders ranging from Parkinson's and heart disease to diabetes and even spinal-cord injury

The Process

1 EMBRYO An egg is fertilized or cloned to form an embryo. The embryo begins to divide

2 1 TO 5 DAYS The embryo divides into more and more cells and forms a hollow ball of cells called a blastocyst

3 5 TO 7 DAYS Embryonic stem cells begin to form along the inside of the blastocyst, creating the inner cell mass

able to differentiate ESCs reliably enough that they could be safely transplanted into people, although animal studies with human cells are under way.

The groups closest to human trials are in the biotech industry, which operates without government funds. One firm, Geron, claims it is close to filing for permission to conduct the first human trials relying on ESC-based therapy. It is using stem cells to create oligodendroglial progenitor cells, which produce neurons and provide myelin insulation for the long fingers that extend out from the body of a nerve cell. Dr. Lanza of Advanced Cell Technology hopes to file for FDA permission to begin clinical trials on three cell-based therapies: one for macular degeneration, one for repairing heart muscle and another for regenerating damaged skin.

But the closer scientists come to human trials, the more concerned the FDA will be with ensuring patient safety. The government will look at how the cells were grown and whether there would be risk of contamination from animal products used in the process. Regulators want data on how the cells will behave in the human body. Stem cells have shown a dismaying talent for turning into tumors. Will they migrate into unwanted areas? No one knows, and it's hard to test in humans until you can be reasonably sure you won't harm them in the process.

Even as scientists press ahead with embryo research, exciting news has come from the least controversial sources: the stem cells in umbilical-cord blood and placentas, and even in fully formed adult organs. While not as flexible as embryonic cells, cord and placental cells have proved more valuable than scientists initially hoped. Although about 90% of cord-blood stem cells are precursors for blood and immune cells, the remaining 10% give rise to liver, heart-muscle and brain cells and more. Over the past five years, cord-blood

WHERE THEY COME FROM

LEFTOVER OR DEAD-END IVF EMBRYOS

Why they are useful More than 400,000 embryos created during in vitro fertilization lie frozen in clinic tanks in the U.S. Many of them will be discarded, so the embryonic stem cells that exist inside them could be salvaged

Drawbacks The freezing process may make it harder to extract stem cells. Some of the embryos were the weakest ones created by infertile couples and may not yield high-quality stem cells

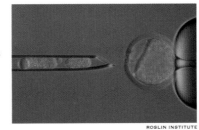

ROSLIN INSTITUTE

◄ NUCLEAR-TRANSFER EMBRYOS

Why they are useful These embryos are created using the technique that created Dolly, the cloned sheep. Stem cells can be custom-made by inserting a patient's skin cell into a hollowed human egg. Any resulting therapies would not run the risk of immune rejection

Drawbacks The process has not yet been successfully completed with human cells, and it requires an enormous amount of fresh human eggs, which are difficult to obtain

GARY D. GAUGLER—PHOTOTAKE

◄ ADULT STEM CELLS

Why they are useful They exist in many major tissues, including the blood, skin and brain. They can be coaxed to produce more cells of a specific lineage and do not have to be extracted from embryos

Drawbacks They can generate only a limited number of cell types, and they are difficult to grow in culture

UMBILICAL-CORD CELLS ►

Why they are useful Although they are primarily made up of blood stem cells, they also contain stem cells that can turn into bone, cartilage, heart muscle and brain and liver tissue. Like adult stem cells, they are harvested without the need for embryos

Drawbacks An umbilical cord is not very long and doesn't hold enough cells to treat an adult

COLIN CUTHBERT—PHOTO RESEARCHERS

4 STEM LINE
The cells are scraped away and grown on a layer of feeder cells and culture medium

5 TISSUE PRODUCTION
Groups of stem cells are nurtured under specialized conditions, with different recipes of nutrients and growth factors that direct the cells to become any of the body's more than 200 various tissues

◄ Pancreatic islet cells
Could provide a cure for diabetes

Muscle cells
Could repair or replace a damaged heart

▲ Nerve cells
Could be used to treat Parkinson's, spinal-cord injuries and strokes

TIME Graphic

---

transplants have become a popular alternative to bone-marrow transplants for blood disorders.

Adult stem cells are less plastic than cord-blood cells, but until recently researchers thought these cells couldn't do much more than regenerate cell types that reflected the stem cells' origin—blood and immune cells from bone marrow, for example. Even so, some scientists believe adult stem cells may prove to be a powerful source of therapies. "In some cases, you may not want to go all the way back to embryonic stem cells," says Joanne Kurtzberg at the Duke University Medical Center. "You wouldn't want to put a cell in the brain and find out later that it turned into bone."

Researchers in Thailand have taken stem cells from the blood of cardiac patients, grown the cells in a lab and reinjected them into patients' hearts, where they set about repairing damage. Two UCLA researchers published a study in June 2006 demonstrating that they could transform adult stem cells from fat tissue into smooth-muscle cells, which assist in the function of numerous organs. Welcome as the advances are, the subject of adult stem cells is highly political and invites a conflation of real hopes and false ones. "There are papers that have claimed broad uses for certain adult stem cells, and some people say that is sufficient cause to not work on embryonic stem cells," says Owen Witte, director of UCLA's Institute for Stem Cell Biology and Medicine. "Many of those claims were overblown."

Some politicians are calling for a Manhattan Project approach to research, but "biology is more complicated than splitting the atom," Witte says. "The physicists on the Manhattan Project knew what they needed to accomplish and how to measure it. In biology, we're codeveloping our measurement tools and our outcome tools at the same time." Indeed, rather than a massive centralized effort controlled by the Federal Government, the key may be to have the broadest cross section of scientists possible working across the field. When it comes to such an impossibly complicated matter as stem cells, the best role for legislators and Presidents may be neither to steer the science nor to stall it but to stand aside and let it breathe—and thrive. ■

A Deadly Mudslide in the Philippines

In the province of Southern Leyte in the Philippines, a series of deluges that lasted for 10 days was followed by a minor earthquake (magnitude 2.6). But the tremor was enough to send an enormous mudslide pouring down a mountain slope on Feb. 17, burying the town of Guinsaugon, home to some 2,500 people. Above, rescue workers seek survivors, but few in the path of the muck lived. The final death toll: more than 1,000.

A New Discovery in the Valley of the Kings

In February, archaeologists announced the discovery of a new tomb, labeled KV63, in Egypt's Valley of the Kings, that sheltered seven coffins. Egypt's dean of antiquities, Zahi Hawass (see Science Faces) claimed one coffin might contain King Tutankhamen's mother Queen Kiya. But when the coffin, above, was opened, it contained no mummy— and no Mummy. Instead it was filled with ancient embalming materials, strips of linen and funerary garlands.

Meet the Fishapod, an Aquatic Missing Link

The dinofish—or the fishapod, if you prefer— is a critter that grew to at least 9 ft. in length and lived some 375 million years ago, just at the point in evolutionary history when fish were giving rise to the four-legged animals known as tetrapods. And indeed, this creature was a little of each, for along with a fish's scales, fangs and gills, it had anatomical features usually found only in animals that spend at least some of their time on land, including a rudimentary hand. It is, in short, just the sort of transitional animal Darwinian theory predicts. The remains of the beast, named *Tiktaalik roseae,* were found by University of Chicago paleontologist Neil Shubin on Canada's Ellesmere Island in 2005 but made public in 2006.

Pacific Apertures

A major undersea earthquake some 6 miles southwest of Hawaii's "Big Island" roused citizens from their slumbers at 7:07 a.m. on Oct. 15, and the ground continued to rumble with a series of aftershocks after the 6.6 quake had passed. Fortunately, there was no loss of life, although homes, churches (right) and schools were damaged and a number of injuries were reported. The misery extended to the sister islands of Oahu and Maui, where power outages occurred. Hawaiians dodged a bullet when the state's biggest earthquake since 1983 generated only a small tsunami wave, measured at 4 in. "We were rocking and rolling ... swaying back and forth," resident Anne LaVasseur told the Associated Press, "like King Kong's pushing your house back and forth."

AGUSTIN TABARES—AP/WIDE WORLD

MARCIO JOSE SANCHEZ—AP/WIDE WORLD

NASA

New Power for the Space Station

Astronaut Joseph Tanner, a NASA mission specialist, performs a repair job, above, on the International Space Station during a 12-day September flight of the space shuttle *Atlantis.* After successfully docking with the station, the six-person *Atlantis* crew delivered the first major new component to be added to it since 2002, a giant truss the size of a school bus and weighing 35,000 lbs. The 45-ft.-long truss holds a solar array at each end, which eventually will provide more than a quarter of the space station's power. The light-gathering wings of the arrays were later extended to their full 240-ft. extent.

Astronaut Steve MacLean became the first Canadian to operate the shuttle's complex, Canadian-built robotic arm, which played a key role in the successful deployment of the arrays. One sour note: critics continue to call the space station an overpriced waste of research funds.

> " This is not some archaic branch of the animal kingdom. This is our branch. You're looking at your great-great-great-great cousin! "
>
> —NEIL SHUBIN, *the University of Chicago paleontologist who discovered the remains of* Tiktaalik roseae, *omitting a generation or two*

Fat Models? Slim Chance

It's not news that the models who slink down the world's fashion runways are seldom in need of liposuction. But in 2006 the health of these splendid splinters did make news, when authorities in Spain banned underweight models from the Madrid fashion shows following the death of a South American model after a show. TIME's Belinda Luscombe blamed the skinny trend on models' steady diet of "nicotine, arugula and rock-star boyfriends."

JOHN D. MCHUGH—AFP—GETTY IMAGES

Health Briefs

In one of the nation's least-expected food scares of recent years, packages of California spinach on sale around the country were tainted with *E. coli.* Three people died in September, and more than 200 others in 26 states became ill after eating the vegetable. As of Nov. 1, federal agents were investigating to determine if charges against growers should be filed.

In other health news this year:

● **Inhalable Insulin** In January the FDA approved the first inhalable insulin, Pfizer's Exubera. Experts hope the user-friendly alternative to injections will encourage wider use of insulin by diabetics.

● **Cervical Cancer Vaccine** In June the FDA approved Gardasil, the first vaccine against most cases of cervical cancer. One concern: at $360 for three shots given over six months, the price tag puts it out of reach of many women in the U.S. and abroad.

● **Sodas Banned from Schools** The Clinton Foundation, run by the former President, the American Heart Association and the three biggest beverage makers in the U.S.—Coke, Pepsi and Cadbury Schweppes—teamed up in May to announce an agreement to kick high-calorie, sugary drinks out of school vending machines and replace them with healthier bottled water, unsweetened fruit juices, low-fat milk and sugar-free sodas—all in smaller portions. Studies show that 17% of U.S. students and 66% of adults are overweight or obese.

The Arts

An Industrial Look for a 21st Century Dream Factory

For more than four decades the Guthrie Theater in Minneapolis, Minn., has been one of the nation's leading regional theaters. In 2006 the company moved into a new home on a hilltop overlooking the Mississippi River designed by French architect Jean Nouvel. The $125 million building confirms Minneapolis' position as a showcase for new architecture: it joins new cultural centers in the city designed by Michael Graves, Cesar Pelli and the team of Jacques Herzog and Pierre de Meuron. The indigo metal box deliberately resembles aging factories and grain silos along the river. "It was important to me to create a link with the history of the city," Nouvel told TIME critic Richard Lacayo. "Theater is an industry too."

new Guthrie Theater building, on the large photos of playwrights and past productions in its lobby

Johnny Depp

"With any part you play, there is a certain amount of yourself in it ... otherwise, it's just not acting. It's lying." —Depp

Hollywood's Campiest Pirate Waives the Rules

FOR YEARS, ACTOR JOHNNY DEPP WAS KNOWN FOR PLAYING outsiders and eccentrics in offbeat films: it would be difficult to name three more outlandish roles than his Edward Scissorhands (1990), weirdo horror-film director Ed Wood (1994) and Ichabod Crane in *Sleepy Hollow* (1999). But a funny thing happened in 2004 to the former teen idol, who starred in the '80s on TV's *21 Jump Street:* he won a huge audience in a mass-market Hollywood block-buster, *Pirates of the Caribbean: The Curse of the Black Pearl.* Depp's hilarious turn as the swishy, tongue-in-cheek pirate Captain Jack Sparrow was so off-kilter that Walt Disney Pictures executives feared a disaster before the film was released. But moviegoers loved Sparrow, the film was a hit, and Depp received an Oscar nomination for the role. The fun of the performance only increased when Depp confessed he had modeled his woozy buccaneer on a friend, legendary Rolling Stones guitarist Keith Richards.

Depp returned as Sparrow in the biggest hit of 2006, *Pirates of the Caribbean: Dead Man's Chest,* although this time director Gore Verbinski laid on so many special effects that the actor was overshadowed. Even so, Depp now occupies a position his peers must envy: he can still pursue the bizarre roles he loves and will return to the gold mine for a third *Pirates* installment, due in the summer of 2007.

Depp claims his body bears the marks of self-abuse from his childhood; he grew up in a painful family situation. The actor shuns the Hollywood scene for the quiet life in France with his partner, French actress Vanessa Paradis, and their two young children. There's a good deal of the raffish Sparrow in the actor, who plays rock guitar, has had several run-ins with the law and sports 13 tattoos: after breaking up with actress Winona Ryder, he altered his WINONA FOREVER tattoo to read WINO FOREVER. Depp was a close friend of Hunter S. Thompson, the gonzo journalist he portrayed in 1998's *Fear and Loathing in Las Vegas.* In 2007 Depp will bring the macabre to the multiplex mob once again when he stars in the title role of a filmed version of Stephen Sondheim's Broadway musical hit, *Sweeney Todd.* ■

The Masked Marvel

ACTORS IDENTIFY TWO STARKLY DIFFERENT ways of approaching their characters. Some, like British great Sir Laurence Olivier, work from the outside in, first finding a look, voice, walk and gestures for their character, then probing their emotions. Since the 1950s heyday of the Method school, many American actors have preferred to work from the inside out, attempting to locate and embody the emotional core of their character and letting the exterior trappings follow.

Meryl Streep, who has reigned over the U.S. stage and screen for a quarter-century now, is of the Olivier school: a master of faces and dialects, she has thrilled audiences as a Victorian Briton in *The French Lieutenant's Woman* (1981), as a Polish Holocaust survivor in *Sophie's Choice* (1982), and as an Australian mother in *A Cry in the Dark* (1988).

In 2006 Streep, 57 and the mother of four children, added two more strong portrayals to her hall of masks. In the movie *The Devil Wears Prada*, she avoided modeling her look on that of the villain of Lauren Weisberger's roman á clef, *Vogue* editor Anna Wintour. Instead, Streep turned her locks gray, her looks icy and her demeanor brittle as she brought fashion editor and emotional dominatrix Miranda Priestly to prickly life. TIME critic Richard Schickel summed up her performance as "predictably, a marvel."

In the summer Streep took on a tougher role, commandeering the New York Shakespeare Festival's Central Park outdoor stage as the title character in Bertolt Brecht's grim 1939 epic of life during the Thirty Years War, *Mother Courage and Her Children*. Wearing a jaunty if tattered cap, Streep appeared in almost every scene of the 3-hr. play, carrying the show on her shoulders. It was another triumph for the woman who, after winning an acting award, once asked her longtime makeup artist Roy Helland to keep doing "his best to destroy my natural good looks." ■

Meryl Streep

"Meryl made the decision. She and Roy [makeup artist Roy Helland] sent us a photo and said, 'Here's the look.'"
—David Frankel, director of *The Devil Wears Prada*

Ledgerdemain: Hollywood Conjures Up a New Star

TALK ABOUT A TRIPLE WHAMMY: ANY ONE OF THE THREE adjectives in the phrase "gay western art film" would normally spell box-office doom for a U.S. movie. Yet director Ang Lee's gay western art film *Brokeback Mountain* became the most discussed film of 2006, after debuting in only six cities in December 2005 in order to make the deadline for '06 Oscar consideration. The film's breakaway star was Heath Ledger, 27, who was nominated for best actor honors at both the Golden Globes and Oscar ceremonies. Ledger won neither award, but that didn't dim the growing star power of the Australian, who first came to American moviegoers' attention playing Mel Gibson's son in *The Patriot* (2000). Ledger also played a medieval heartthrob in *A Knight's Tale* (2001) and starred in the title role of *Ned Kelly* (2003), the saga of Australia's outlaw folk hero.

As Ennis Del Mar in *Brokeback Mountain,* Ledger was saddled with the tough assignment of playing a man completely out of touch with his own emotions, for whom uttering an entire sentence seems a, well, back-breaking challenge. Yet despite his character's drawling, mumbling and aw-shucksing ways, Ledger managed to create a compelling portrait of a classic cowboy loner. New York *Times* critic Stephen Holden declared, "Ledger magically and mysteriously disappears beneath the skin of his lean, sinewy character."

Shortly after *Brokeback* rode into the multiplex sunset, audiences who might have assumed Ledger was only a he-man type got a shock when he starred as the lusty 18th century title character in Lasse Hallstrom's *Casanova.* Bewigged, bemasked and bemused, Ledger made for a convincing Venetian courtier, whose nimble witticisms were a long way from Del Mar's clench-jawed one-liners. In private life, Hollywood's latest "it" boy, who once dated fellow Australian Naomi Watts, is now engaged to his *Brokeback* co-star Michelle Williams, with whom he had a daughter, Matilda Rose, in 2005. Coming in 2008 to a theater near you: Ledger plays Jack Nicholson's role as the Joker in the next Batman epic, *The Dark Knight.* ∎

Heath Ledger

"There's nothing girly about Ledger's Ennis Del Mar. He's classic cowboy ... he doesn't have too much to say, but he's got a Russian novel's worth of body language."—TIME critic Belinda Luscombe

Paying Attention to the Man Behind the Curtain

WHEN NEW YORK CITY'S METROPOLITAN OPERA, LONG THE nation's flagship company, opened its 2006 season on Sept. 25 with a new production of Puccini's *Madama Butterfly*, the man feeling the most butterflies was probably the new general manager of the Met, Peter Gelb. Named in 2005 to the position once held by the legendary Rudolph Bing and for the past 16 years by the gritty Joseph Volpe, Gelb, 52, first worked in the house as a part-time usher in high school; he later produced telecasts of Met performances. Before being tapped to head the Met, Gelb made a reputation as an innovator as the head of Sony Classical Records, where he succeeded in bringing serious music to wider audiences by pairing classical and mainstream artists and creating fresh marketing strategies that helped blow the dusty reputation off the music of the masters.

Gelb hopes to work the same magic at the Met, which, like all U.S. classical music companies, is faced with high production costs, aging audiences and the need to attract new, younger listeners. He wasted no time in showing that the Met had entered a new era, canceling a Three Tenors concert planned for the 2006 opening-night gala in favor of the new staging of *Butterfly* directed by filmmaker Anthony Minghella. Gelb also said the Met would cut the price of its cheapest tickets and sell 200 orchestra seats each night for only $20; formerly the cheapest such seat cost $100. Next on Gelb's list: live nationwide Met simulcasts in local movie theaters and broadcasts on Sirius satellite radio. On opening night, the Met audience included comedian Jimmy Fallon, actor Jude Law and rocker David Bowie—proof that a hip new crowd is welcoming Gelb's ch-ch-ch-changes. ∎

Peter Gelb

"The same person who loves a sophisticated Broadway musical should also love a great opera. What has been missing is ... a campaign to educate the broader public that opera is, at its best, a wonderful alchemy of music and theater." —Gelb

Hearst Tower In the 1920s, publishing mogul William Randolph Hearst built the six-story masonry base from which Norman Foster's 46-story skyscraper now sprouts. Hearst planned to erect a taller building in the future, but the Depression intervened. Eighty-some years later, the Hearst Co. hired Foster to realize its founder's dream. The building's webwork of triangular structural modules, called a diagrid, is far more stable than typical vertical supports, and it offers a complex skein of surfaces to reflect the constant change of natural light. Because the diagrid divides the building into four-story segments, it provides a human scale that an unbroken glass-curtain wall could not.

Thinking Out of the Box

A trio of modern masters tackles the challenge of wedding old buildings to new, and the result is a burst of fresh forms and a celebration of light

FOR TODAY'S CELEBRITY ARCHITECTS AND THOSE WHO PAY their extravagant fees, the Big Bang isn't something that occurred a long time ago in a galaxy far, far away: it went off in a blast of titanium when American Frank Gehry's Guggenheim Museum in Bilbao, Spain, opened its doors in 1997. For patrons with deep pockets and high expectations, Gehry's futuristic building sounded a reveille: the age of the Modernist box was history, and the shape of the future was, well, anything but a Modernist box. For the boards of major museums, symphony halls and media companies, hiring an internationally renowned architect to confer instant status on a new building project is now de rigueur.

That's not to complain about the fresh wave of imaginative buildings that is continuing to redefine city centers around the world, including the three pictured here, Briton Norman Foster's Hearst Tower, Italian Renzo Piano's addition to the Morgan Library and Museum (both in New York City) and Pole Daniel Libeskind's Denver Art Museum. Each of them offers a fascinating conversation between older buildings and the new aesthetic, for in all three cases the architect was asked to create an addition to an already standing edifice.

Mastery of light is another unifying theme in the buildings. Foster's buildings are always environmentally conscious; the Hearst Tower centers on a huge indoor piazza, a 10-story atrium bathed in sunlight from skylights high above. Libeskind's Denver Art Museum gets around curators' understandable fear of direct sunlight by drawing in Colorado's glowing natural light from a 120-ft.-high central atrium that indirectly illuminates adjacent galleries. And Piano's soaring glass atrium, located between the stolid masonry of the old Morgan Library and his new addition, weds the hushed spaces of the museum to New York City's bustling streets. ■

Denver Art Museum Daniel Libeskind's jagged, careening angles are a sharp contrast to the museum's old building, designed by Italian Gio Ponti, which opened in 1971. TIME critic Richard Lacayo called the older building "an armor-plated canister" but termed Libeskind's new, $90 million titanium-clad structure "a route to a powerful new model of space and form."

Morgan Library and Museum Renzo Piano was given the difficult task of unifying three existing buildings: the 1906 Morgan Library, a 1928 annex building and the mid–19th century Morgan House. Piano delved deep into the ground to create new spaces for concerts and collections, opened up new galleries with large windows and unified it all with the transparent atrium at right.

Run for Your Lives! The Blockbusters Are Here!

Every summer, Hollywood bids a farewell to charms and unleashes a barrage of special effects upon the nation's innocent multiplexes

COMING NEXT SUMMER TO A THEATER NEAR YOU: MORE OF the freakin' same! Since Steven Spielberg invented the hot-weather blockbuster with *Jaws*, way back in 1975, summertime at the cinema has brought a plethora of sequels, prequels and remakes, generally laden with so many special effects as to rival the popcorn in the lobby for fat content. That leaves little room for emotional stories. As TIME critic Richard Corliss complained, "Young American males— the most avidly courted summer movie audience—get all tense and nervous when they see a man and a woman (or, for that matter, a boy and a girl) get down to consequential love-

making. It is tiresome to be held in constant thrall to their immaturity. I know there are profits to be made from this kind of filmmaking, but I don't think the movies can really prosper unless they reconnect with their romantic roots, tell us at least a few stories of love lost and found, squandered and redeemed." Amen to that. In the meantime, here are the films teenage males loved best in the summer of 2006. ∎

$421 million

❶ Pirates of the Caribbean: Dead Man's Chest Johnny Depp was back as Captain Jack Sparrow in the sequel to Disney's monster 2004 summer hit, and that was all audiences needed to know. Overlong, overstuffed with special effects and just plain over the top, Gore Verbinski's film made subtlety walk the plank.
TIME ["It] proves, once again, that special effects aren't funny and brilliant performances aren't always repeatable."

Source: Boxofficemojo.com; U.S. domestic grosses only

`$244 million`

2 Cars Director John Lasseter of Pixar, which sold its pioneering computer-graphics animation shop to the Walt Disney Co. in 2006, enjoyed another big hit with this original story of a lovable NASCAR wannabe and his autocentric world.
TIME "... straddling the realms of Pixar styling and old Disney heart, this new-model Cars is an instant classic."

`$217 million`

4 The Da Vinci Code The film adaptation of Dan Brown's ultra-popular novel did well at the U.S. box office and was a huge hit abroad, but critics dissed its length and bemoaned the lack of romantic sparks between stars Tom Hanks and France's Audrey Tatou.
TIME "The result is a work that is politically brave, for a mainstream movie, and artistically stodgy."

`$234 million`

3 X-Men: The Last Stand We strongly doubt that this is the last stand for this highly successful franchise, whose ongoing tale of mutants vs. humans provides Hugh Jackman, Kelsey Grammer and Halle Berry, above, with one-dimensional superhero starring roles while offering up lots of computerized scenery for British thespians Ian McKellen and Patrick Stewart to chew on.
TIME "How many distinguished veterans of the Royal Shakespeare Company does it take to make a big-budget trashy movie? Well, two."

`$199 million`

5 Superman Returns The Man of Steel bounded back onto the big screen after a long layoff; relative unknown Brandon Routh donned the tights, while Kevin Spacey took over as villain Lex Luthor.
TIME "The[movie] is an action adventure that's as thrilling for what it means as for what it shows"

Old Wine, New Bottles

A chipper cook and a bogus broadcaster liven up TV screens, while an aging enigma and a tough Texas trio release strong new albums

Rachael Ray

Move over, Katie Couric: now that you're polishing your gravitas as the new anchor of the CBS evening newscast, your former title as the Perkiest Woman on the Tube has passed to America's most frenzied foodie, Rachael Ray. This Prospero of the kitchen island is down-home (sample expression: "easy peasy"), down with everyday recipes (meatloaf, anyone?) but also relentlessly upbeat. In the fall of 2006, Ray launched a syndicated talk show, even as she was starring in four different programs on the Food Network: *30-Minute Meals, $40 a Day, Inside Dish* and *Rachael Ray's Tasty Travels*. In her spare time, the 38-year-old has launched a magazine and written a best-selling series of cookbooks featuring her accelerated approach to meal preparation, designed for people who are almost as busy as she is. Ray, whose first job was working the candy counter at Macy's in New York City, married lawyer John Cusimano in 2005 in Tuscany. Tasty!

The Dixie Chicks

STICKS NIX DIXIE CHICKS. That *Variety*-style headline sums up the recent travails of the trio whose infectious country sound made lead singer Natalie Maines (center, below) and sisters Martie Maguire and Emily Robison (left and right) the best-selling female act in pop-music history. But in March 2003, just before U.S. troops entered Iraq, Maines told a London audience, "Just so you know, we're ashamed the President of the United States is from Texas." Bad career move: true-blue patriotism is the only acceptable political stance among country-music fans. Soon records were banned on radio stations, names were called, death threats were issued, and the Chicks' career went flat.

In 2006 the tart trio released their first CD since the London comment. TIME's Josh Tyrangiel hailed *Taking the Long Way*: "it may be the best adult-pop CD of the year." The new CD sold well, but many country fans boycotted it. The album got little play by once adoring radio DJs, and concerts in some Southern cities were canceled. Said Tyrangiel: "By gambling their careers, three Texas women have the biggest balls in American music."

Stephen Colbert

In a media-saturated world, Stephen Colbert practices an art form that might be described as meta-TV. On *The Colbert Report,* the Comedy Central spin-off of his work on Jon Stewart's *The Daily Show,* the host, 42, expertly parodies the puffed-up personalities who dominate TV's news programs. Writing for TIME's 100 Most Influential People issue in 2006, NBC bigfoot Brian Williams called him "the bawdy counterweight to cable-news talking heads who each night, just a few channels away, deliver a fresh supply of material for parody." After *The Colbert Report's* fall 2005 debut, its host hit paydirt by coining the term "truthiness" to describe the media's increasing Photoshopping of reality. Commentators seized upon the word to describe the rush of fake memoirs and plagiarized novels that appeared in 2006. Colbert's truth-to-power speech at the White House Correspondents' Association Dinner in 2006 offended both guest President Bush and his hosts but became a YouTube classic.

Bob Dylan

America's cranky Cassandra may be 65, but Bob Dylan continues to enjoy a late-career upswing that has brought the reclusive artist more into the open than at any other time in his long career. In 2006 Dylan scored his first No. 1 record on the charts since 1976's *Desire* with *Modern Times*. The title of the new effort was a typically deadpan joke from the songwriter. All its 12 cuts sounded as if they could have been recorded anytime between 1940 and 2006, and the titles were equally preowned: *Rollin' and Tumblin'*, *When the Deal Goes Down*, *Workingman's Blues #2*. But Dylan's lyrical mastery and unique vocal phrasing made the album the third in a series of late-career triumphs that includes *Time Out of Mind* (1997) and *Love and Theft* (2001). As an author, Dylan is still riding a wave of good reviews for his revelatory 2004 memoir, *Chronicles Vol. 1*.

How does Dylan stay forever young? In 2006 he starred in a TV commercial for today's hottest music accessory, the Apple iPod, and he continued his relentless round of live performances, dubbed the Never-Ending Tour, often featuring hip young artists like the Raconteurs as opening acts. But Dylan's most impressive performance in 2006 came in a newfangled version of an old-fashioned medium. On his *Theme Time Radio Hour* on XM Satellite Radio, the gravel-voiced elder took fans on fascinating musical search parties, with each program centered on an inviting theme: baseball, mothers, drinking, the weather. Dusting off seldom-heard musical oddities, sharing illuminating insights and offbeat personal anecdotes, Dylan turned his weekly 60 minutes into a hipster's seminar on America's music and its legacy.

WILLIAM CLAXTON

The Bygone Blues

The Great White Way's recipe for hits: familiar movie stars, familiar pop songs, familiar Disney films—and a few revivals

BROADWAY PRODUCERS KNOW THERE IS A HUGE DEMAND for their wares: a big hit can play for years in New York City, spawn productions in major cities around the world and send a host of traveling companies on the road, even while spinning off CDs, film versions, T shirts and refrigerator magnets. And Broadway had a very successful 2005-06 season, taking in a record $861 million. Yes, the audiences are out there—but producers are still struggling to find the magic formula to get them inside the theater.

The year on Broadway brought more of the same tactics that have proved successful in recent years. Once again, stars from other media were imported to add marquee glamour: pop star Usher made a suave Billy Flynn in *Chicago*, but critics dissed Julia Roberts' stiff performance in Richard Greenberg's 1997 drama, *Three Days of Rain*—and what was old *Friend* David Schwimmer doing in the chestnut *The Caine Mutiny Court Martial*? Once again, Disney turned two of its old films, *Tarzan* and *Mary Poppins*, into special-effects extravaganzas. And once again, producers turned to tried-and-true hits from the past in hopes of dazzling new audiences: *A Chorus Line*, *The Pajama Game* and *The Threepenny Opera* were dusted off and successfully shocked into fresh life.

Producers also continued to ransack the pop-culture attic for new "jukebox musicals," the genre in which a cheesy, tongue-in-cheek story is draped with old pop hits. The model is *Mamma Mia!*, the 1999 monster hit based on Abba songs. The year 2006 brought a Johnny Cash musical, *Ring of Fire*; a Twyla Tharp dance-musical set to Bob Dylan songs, *The Times They Are A-Changin'*; and a John Lennon musical biography, *Lennon*. Unlike the 2005 hit *Jersey Boys*, which recalled the glory days of Frankie Valli and the Four Seasons, none of the new jukebox offerings clicked—and all of them proved that on Broadway, the times, they aren't a-changin'. ∎

Tarzan: Disney's new stage version of its 1999 animated film about the famous ape-man plays more like a theme-park ride than a Broadway musical. But Bob Crowley's production—lush vine forests, undulating waters, shape-shifting plants—as well as its cool aerial choreography, makes *Tarzan* an enthralling spectacle

The Drowsy Chaperone: Its premise—poking fun at corny old musicals—has become a corny old device in itself, but the show's cheery, self-mocking inventiveness was irresistible. Sutton Foster, in a knockout number, spins plates, does cartwheels and performs other crowd pleasers while singing "I don't wanna show off"

Mary Poppins: A huge hit in London since its debut in December 2004, the new stage version of the 1964 Disney film classic opened on Broadway in November 2006, featuring wind-borne nannies, cute kids and a roof full of dancing chimney sweeps, as seen in this picture from the British production

The History Boys: British playwright Alan Bennett's comedy-drama about a class of public school boys and their lovably old-fashioned teacher's battles with a charismatic rival was a hit with most critics, but not TIME's Richard Zoglin, who declared, "[It] struck me as a sentimental, highfalutin' version of *Welcome Back, Kotter*."

The Wedding Singer: Hitching a ride on a wave of (believe it or not) '80s nostalgia, the new jukebox musical is based on the 1998 Adam Sandler film. Audiences made it a success, but TIME's Zoglin called its score forgettable and said, "The show winks at the audience so relentlessly... that eventually you just tune out."

ArtsNotes

Step Right Up! Lincoln Center's Human Snowglobe

Magician David Blaine, 33, is out to revive the age of P.T. Barnum and Houdini. So far, he's dangled in a clear box above the Thames in London for 44 days, been frozen in a block of ice in Times Square, been buried in a glass coffin for seven days. This year the staid crew at New York City's Lincoln Center rented out their plaza for the showman's latest stunt: he was submerged, in chains, in a glass ball for seven days, then tried to break the world record for holding his breath underwater on live TV. His breath gave out at the 7-min. 8-sec. mark, 110 sec. shy of the record. No problem: success in such events is really measured by their ability to garner media attention. So … score this one: Blaine 1, TIME Annual 0.

A Nobel Prize for Turkey's Outspoken Writer

The novels of Orhan Pamuk, Turkey's most distinguished writer of fiction, reflect his nation's struggle with its dual identity, part Western, part Islamic. So controversial is Pamuk in his native land that criminal charges, since dropped, were brought against him in 2005, after he discussed the Turkish genocide of Armenians in 1915-17. But his novels have been hailed around the world, and on Oct. 12, Pamuk was awarded the 2006 Nobel Prize for Literature.

Ripping Yarns: Picasso Goes to Las Vegas

Today's Las Vegas is a glittering lure for those eager not only to roll the dice but also to dine in the restaurants of renowned chefs, take in a $150 Cirque du Soleil show and maybe even gaze upon a famous painting or three. Enter Steve Wynn, 64, the hotelier who has shepherded Vegas on its upscale journey, in part by displaying his notable collection of fine art to tourists. This year Wynn agreed to sell *La Rêve,* Pablo Picasso's 1932 portrait of his mistress Marie-Thérèse Walter, for $139 million. But as Wynn, whose vision is impaired, showed the painting to friends, he inadvertently put his elbow through the canvas. The painting will be restored, but the sale is off—house rules.

In the Land of the Tube, *Idol* Rules

Yes, we know: *American Idol* is old news. But the British import that updated the amateur contest show—a Fox-TV hit since its debut as a summer replacement in 2002—enjoyed its most successful season yet in 2006. The show, whose fifth contest aired in the spring, now qualifies as a phenomenon: a record audience watched the final episode on May 24, in which host Ryan Seacrest, left, announced that Taylor Hicks had been voted champion. Katharine McPhee, center, finished second. A surprise guest artist: Prince.

Further proof of the show's starmaking power can be found on the pop-music charts, where former winners and runners-up, including Clay Aiken, Ruben Studdard, Fantasia Barrino and Kelly Clarkson, continue to enjoy strong sales. At this rate, *Idol* may just run forever.

KEVORK DJANSEZIAN—AP/WIDE WORLD

Oprah, James Frey and "Truthiness"

For the chattering classes, the word that defined 2006 was TV wit Stephen Colbert's coinage "truthiness," which captured the doctoring of reality that has become increasingly common in recent years, from political spin to enhanced photographs of Lebanon war scenes to plagiarized novels. The year's most celebrated battle between truth and truthiness involved James Frey's 2003 book, *A Million Little Pieces,* which was presented as a memoir detailing the writer's excessive substance abuse and the traumas that resulted. Talk-show queen Oprah Winfrey had previously selected the book for her popular TV book club. But in January, the Smoking Gun website challenged Frey's veracity, offering evidence to show that his book was more a work of fiction than an autobiography. Winfrey initially defended the writer, calling into a Larry King show featuring Frey to offer support. But two weeks later Winfrey reversed herself, calling the writer onstage with her on her daily show and castigating him for duping her. Memo to memoirists: Don't mess with Oprah.

> **"** Oprah should kick James Frey's bony, lying, nonfiction butt out of the kingdom of Oprah. **"**
>
> —**MAUREEN DOWD,**
> *New York Times columnist,*
> *weighing in on the brouhaha*
> *that followed the revelation that*
> *Frey had falsified events in the*
> *book he presented as a memoir,*
> A Million Little Pieces

All You Need Is Cirque

Steve Wynn, whose run-in with a Picasso masterpiece is detailed at left, brought museum-quality art to Las Vegas. He also helped pioneer the city's production of over-the-top spectacles, a perfect match for its "Astonish me!" audience. On June 30 the Montreal-based Cirque du Soleil company, whose high-flying, high-energy, high-cost shows have set new standards for theatrical spectacle, opened their new $150 million effort at Wynn's Mirage Hotel. *Love* was set to the music of the Beatles, remixed into a swirling, Ivesian 90-min. montage of sound by the group's legendary producer George Martin, now 80. TIME's Richard Corliss, long a fan of the Cirque approach, called the show "the definitive Beatles reunion … a mesmerizing form of sorcery in motion."

JAE C. HONG—AP/WIDE WORLD

LEFT: STEPHEN CHEMIN—AP/WIDE WORLD; RIGHT: NO CREDIT

Milestones

"He left this world in a peaceful and happy state of mind. He would have said, 'Crocs rule!'" — Nature

Down Under's Over-the-Top Hero

Yes, he was bumptious, a bit clumsy and a scenery-chewing ham. Yes, he deployed his buzzword "Crikey!" long past its sell-by date. Yes, the Crocodile Hunter played a khaki-clad parody of himself and his fellow Australians on his familiar TV shows. But Steve Irwin's heart-on-his-sleeve love affair with animals and the natural world was absolutely contagious, especially for the young people everywhere who looked up to him as an Indiana Jones of zoology, a living emblem of the allure and importance of the wild. Irwin, only 44 and the father of two children, was killed when a stingray's barb pierced his heart on Sept. 4 while he was filming off Australia's Batt Reef. The news saddened the world; it was a death in the human family.

1941-2006

Slobodan Milosevic: Brutal Architect of Ethnic Cleansing

WHAT A LEGACY: THE FIRST SENTENCE OF MANY OF THE obituaries of Slobodan Milosevic—the wily, charismatic, power-addicted former Yugoslav President and icon of Serbian nationalism—contained the words "Butcher of the Balkans." Most of them went on to point out that Milosevic was responsible for popularizing an Orwellian term that has entered the language as a synonym for genocide, "ethnic cleansing." Milosevic, who was suffering from heart trouble, died while on trial at the International Criminal Tribunal in the Hague since 2002 for his alleged role as architect of the 1995 slaughter of 8,000 Bosnian Muslims in Srebrenica and other crimes.

Son of a defrocked Orthodox priest and a teacher, Milosevic was a communist economist and banker early in his career; frequent travels to New York City and Paris made him fluent in English and French. He came to power in Serbia in 1989, as a wave of ethnic fervor swept through the fractious republics that composed the federation of Yugoslavia. Energizing long-dormant Serbian nationalism in powerful speeches, Milosevic cultivated the sizable Serb populations of Croatia, Kosovo and Bosnia and Herzegovina, leading to a series of bloody ethnic and religious wars.

U.S. President Bill Clinton and British Prime Minister Tony Blair led a NATO bombing campaign that rolled back Serbia's aggressive intervention in Kosovo in 1999, and Milosevic finally lost power in a 2000 election. Serbia's new leaders extradited him to the Netherlands in 2001. He chose to defend himself at his trial, defiant to the end. ∎

The activist in 1967

1927-2006

Coretta Scott King: Keeper of the Flame

AFTER HER HUSBAND, CIVIL-RIGHTS PIONEER MARTIN Luther King Jr., was murdered while standing on a motel balcony in Memphis, Tenn., on April 4, 1968, Coretta Scott King hid her grief, shielded her four children from the media and immediately took up his campaign for racial equality. Before his burial she flew to Memphis to take his place at the head of a march by garbage collectors striking for better wages, the cause that had brought the Rev. King to the city. In the days that followed, she appeared at other protests to echo his message and calm enraged supporters.

Keeping her eyes on the prize—guarding her husband's legacy—King became one of the most revered figures of the modern civil-rights movement. She led a 15-year push that succeeded in 1983 in establishing a federal holiday in her husband's honor, founded the King Center for Nonviolent Social Change in Atlanta and traveled the world in support of civil-rights issues, including same-sex marriage. A long-time foe of apartheid, she shared the stage with Nelson Mandela when he was sworn in as President of South Africa in 1994.

King's conduct was controversial at times; critics accused her and her children of exploiting the Rev. King's writings for profit, and she was criticized by some for her efforts in the late 1990s to secure a new trial for James Earl Ray, who was convicted of assassinating her husband. (She believed, as did some others, that Ray was probably innocent and King's murder was the work of several conspirators.) Her primary achievement, though, was in turning her husband's mission into her own, saying "Hate is too great a burden "

The former Governor in 2000

Ann Richards: Lone Star Great

SALTY, SASSY, QUICK-WITTED AND EMINENTLY QUOTABLE, onetime Texas Governor Ann Richards was a rare bird in modern America's highly partisan political aviary: a committed Democrat who was widely admired by Republicans. In a state where politics had always been a boys' club, Richards earned a place at the table for talking straight, for tackling tough problems and for taking direction from an internal compass rather than poll readings. Her famous poke at Vice President George H.W. Bush at the 1988 Democratic Convention—"Poor George. He was born with a silver foot in his mouth"—prompted talk of a national role for the Texas state treasurer. It also prompted a gift from Bush in the form of a silver charm, shaped like a foot.

Richards raised a family of four and taught school for years before beginning her career in politics on the county commission in the capital city of Austin. She became an effective state treasurer and ended up in the Governor's

mansion in 1991, where she made good on campaign promises to open up the government to those previously excluded, appointing minorities and women in unprecedented numbers to executive positions in the statehouse. On her way to the Governor's mansion, she beat a number of male opponents and a drinking problem. But once in office, she couldn't beat George W. Bush, who ousted her from the governorship in 1995, and she couldn't beat the esophageal cancer that took her life at 73.

TIME asked a fellow Texan, celebrity columnist Liz Smith, to comment on Richards: "I've known every First Lady going back to Eleanor Roosevelt," Smith wrote. "But forget them—and Mother Teresa too. I think Ann Richards was the greatest woman I have ever known. The former Governor of Texas was electrifying, brilliant, loyal, tolerant. She was also exhausting. I am surprised Ann stopped long enough to leave this world."

1921-2006

Betty Friedan: Founding Feminist

S HE WAS BORN IN PEORIA, ILL., TO A MOTHER WHO had quit her newspaper job to be a homemaker. And Betty Friedan herself was once fired after she asked for maternity leave. A lifelong voice from the left, Friedan helped launch the modern feminist movement with her 1963 best seller, *The Feminine Mystique*, which explored the "sense of dissatisfaction" in a mid-century woman who "made the beds, shopped for groceries, matched slipcover material, ate peanut butter sandwiches with her children" while secretly wondering "Is this all?"

Mystique sprang from research Friedan undertook for an article on what had happened to her classmates in Smith College's class of '42. It made her a hero to a generation of educated middle-class women, although by the late 1960s she was regarded by some more radical feminists as outdated; she spoke out firmly against "the bra-burning, anti-man, politics-of-orgasm school [of feminism]." A co-founder of the National Organization for Women and the group later known as the National Abortion Rights Action League, Friedan eventually switched her attention to the plight of older people. Her last book, 1993's *The Fountain of Age*, explored how the aged are patronized in the same way women have often been. ∎

DAVID GAHR

The theorist of gender in 1965

1941-2006

Ed Bradley: Style and Substance

ALTHOUGH HE WAS ALREADY FIGHTING THE LEUKEMIA THAT WOULD claim his life, veteran CBS News correspondent Ed Bradley didn't check into a hospital until his last story for *60 Minutes*, about an explosion at a Texas oil refinery, aired on Oct. 29, 2006. Bradley, a native of Philadelphia, had come a long way since his first day at a New York City news radio station in 1967, where he was one of three black employees (the others were a technician and the janitor). Too talented and too driven to settle for the "black story" beat, Bradley became a renaissance reporter: after signing with CBS in 1971, he covered Vietnam and the White House and spearheaded numerous investigative stories, which landed him a spot on *60 Minutes* a decade later. Equipped with an easy style that disarmed everyone from Oklahoma City bomber Timothy McVeigh to Michael Jackson, Bradley made the show's magazine format sing. This was never truer than in a classic 1981 profile of torch singer Lena Horne, a revealing study of age, race, gender and show biz.

"I've always thought I've had the ability to look at someone, and between 'the look' and the silence, get them to be honest," he said in 1995. "As much as the look, it's the silence that works. When you're interviewing someone and you just wait, they rush to fill that space." Recognized with 20 Emmy Awards, Bradley eschewed the standard blandness of the network bigfoot, suggesting through his ironic asides, salt-and-pepper stubble, dapper dress (and in later years an earring) that he savored life off-camera. A passionate devotee of jazz, he sometimes joined musicians he admired onstage, playing along on tambourine or guitar. Once asked to reflect on his life's work, Bradley replied, "If I arrived at the Pearly Gates and St. Peter said, 'What have you done to deserve entry?' I'd just say, 'Did you see my Lena Horne story?' " ∎

The economist sees double in 1986

1912-2006

Milton Friedman: Prophet of Free Markets

JOHN MAYNARD KEYNES, THE MOST INFLUENTIAL ECONO-mist of the first half of the 20th century, once noted, "Practical men ... are usually the slaves of some defunct economist." Milton Friedman, the most influential econo-mist of the second half of the century, disproved this maxim (along with many other theories by Keynes) by bringing the world around to his point of view while he was still alive.

After World War II, Friedman began espousing the heretical notion that monetary policy, the manipulation of interest rates and the money supply, was the only effective way for governments to influence the economy. In contrast, Keynes and his followers preached the power of fiscal policy, in the form of taxes and government spending. A founder of "the Chicago School," a group of conservative economists headquartered at the University of Chicago, Friedman was derided for years as an eccentric, if brilliant, crank. But his prediction that reliance on fiscal tinkering

would, over time, produce a devastating amalgam of infla-tion and unemployment (an outcome Keynesian economics viewed as impossible) was borne out in the "stagflation" of the 1970s. Friedman won the Nobel Prize in Economics in 1976 and went on to serve as an adviser for Ronald Reagan, Margaret Thatcher and other leaders determined to remake their economies along free-market lines.

It's a rare feat for an intellectual's ideas to resonate in both the ivory tower and the halls of power, yet Friedman accomplished an even more difficult leap. A gifted commu-nicator, he dazzled the general public with a series of best-selling books and a 10-part 1980 PBS series, *Free to Choose*. In preaching the gospel of free markets, he made a related point that was as much political as economic: people, rather than governments, should manage economies through the choices they make—and personal liberty is diminished when the reverse is attempted.

The polymath in 2001

1908-2006

John Kenneth Galbraith: Influential Critic of an Affluent Society

HE WAS BORN IN CANADA, BUT HIS TOWERING HEIGHT—6 ft. 8 in.—his lantern jaw and his air of intellectual distinction made him appear to be a Boston Brahmin, say, the model from which Senator John Kerry was later knocked off. Galbraith indeed landed at Harvard University, and in the days before the nation's political center of gravity shifted from the East Coast to the Sunbelt, he wielded enormous influence as a probing economist, a leading voice of U.S. liberalism and a pithy and outspoken critic of America's status-conscious consumer culture.

Over the course of a long, distinguished career, Galbraith helped set World War II economic guidelines; worked as a journalist at Henry Luce's FORTUNE magazine, taught economics at Harvard for decades; served as John F. Kennedy's ambassador to India; helped engineer Lyndon Johnson's Great Society; and wrote 33 books, including the highly influential 1958 best seller *The Affluent Society*, whose title entered the American language, as did another of his coinages, "conventional wisdom." TIME's critic, however, panned *The Affluent Society*, describing it as "a vague essay with the air of worried dinner-table conversation."

Galbraith was known for his witty, often acerbic tone, once noting, "The only function of economic forecasting is to make astrology look respectable." The concepts in *The Affluent Society* became so pervasive that to subsequent generations of readers, "it's like reading *Hamlet* and deciding it's full of quotations," said Nobel laureate economist Amartya Sen. "You realize where they came from." ∎

PAUL A. SOUNDERS—CORBIS

1954-2006

Susan Butcher: Call of the Wild

S HE WAS BORN IN MASSACHUSETTS, BUT SUSAN BUTCHER headed for the hills as soon as she could. She attended college in Colorado, where she first worked with huskies, but the Rockies were too tame for her. In 1973 she followed her wilderness dreams to Alaska, where she lived for three years in the Wrangell Mountains, sans electricity, sans running water and, for the most part, sans neighbors.

Returning to civilization, Butcher founded Trail Breaker Kennels outside Fairbanks—and proceeded to break some trails herself with four victories in the grueling 1,150-mile-long Iditarod sled-dog race. Butcher, only 5 ft. 6 in. and 135 lbs., put the little-known regional event on the sporting world's map by winning the race four times, including three years in succession (1986, '87, '88) and finishing twice

three times (although in 1985 Libby Riddles earned the distinction of being the first woman to win the race).

Perhaps Butcher's most memorable Iditarod was one she didn't even finish. She was in the lead in 1985 when a moose attacked her sled team, killing two dogs quickly and injuring 13 others. As Butcher told the Los Angeles *Times,* "I held her off with an ax for about 20 minutes, and then another musher came along and shot her." As for her ability to mush with little sleep for 10 or 12 days on the trail, Butcher shared her secret with TIME in 2000: "My favorite thing to do was scoop up a handful of snow and throw it in my face." Butcher, who left behind husband Dave Monson and two daughters, succumbed at 51 to complications of polycythemia vera, a rare blood disease. ∎

The master musher in 1991

William Styron: Cartographer Of Contemporary Morality

ACRAFTSMAN WHO CONSTRUCTED HIS AMBI-tious fictions on a legal pad at a painstaking pace of no more than a page and a half per day, William Styron once claimed, "A great book should leave you with many experiences—and slightly exhausted." His morally provocative epics —including three powerful novels that promise to be read long into the future, *Lie Down in Darkness* (1951), *The Confessions of Nat Turner* (1967) and *Sophie's Choice* (1979)—explore, in agonizing detail, the human capacity for evil.

A descendant of slave owners, Styron became obsessed as a boy with the 1831 slave revolt led by Nat Turner, which began not far from his childhood home in Newport News, Va. *Confessions*, written in the first person, drew bitter criticism from some black leaders, who called it presumptuous; they particularly objected to a scene in which Turner dreams of raping a white woman. But the novel won Styron a Pulitzer Prize. Along with *Sophie's Choice*, the harrowing tale of an Auschwitz survivor that became an Oscar-winning 1982 movie starring Meryl Streep, it cemented his reputation as a literary giant. On its publication, TIME reviewer Paul Gray called it "a sprawling, uneven yet brave attempt to render the unimaginable horror of the Nazi death camps ... He keeps the horror at arm's length, in the past and in another country, but offers a heroine-victim who can forget nothing."

Styron served in uniform in both World War II and the Korean War but did not see combat. In the 1950s he joined a group of U.S. literary exiles in Paris, where he became a co-founder of the influential *Paris Review*. The artist who confronted such outsized evils as slavery and fascism faced internal demons of his own: in 1990 he chronicled his struggle with depression in the memoir *Darkness Visible*, which was hailed as a pioneering work that turned a much needed spotlight on a devastating, once unmentionable disease. ∎

The writer in 1981

1925-2006

Robert Altman:
Whitman of the Screen

The lion in winter, 2006

WORKING AGAINST THE GRAIN IN an age of formulaic filmmaking, director Robert Altman was a prolific, curmudgeonly, irreplaceable renegade whose movies both defined and mocked the modern American spirit. Arriving in Hollywood after flying B-24 bombers in World War II, the native of Kansas City kicked around the industry for nearly a quarter-century before directing *MASH* (1970), a ribald Army comedy set in the Korean War but offering a cynical take on U.S. involvement in Vietnam. *MASH* set the Altman attitude and technique: sprawling frescoes with crawling cameras, dozens of characters, overlapping dialogue and a belief that life was way too messy and complex for ordinary film narratives. Any Western town (*McCabe & Mrs. Miller*), casino (*California Split*), reception (*A Wedding*), concert (*Nashville*), Hollywood power grab (*The Player*), L.A. earthquake (*Short Cuts*) or English country weekend (*Gosford Park*) could be the setting for his artful chaos, which gave actors plenty of freedom—and writers nightmares.

"His fugue format," TIME critic Richard Corliss wrote in an appreciation, "pouring dozens of plots into a post–ethnic melting pot, gave everyone a brief grab at movie immortality

On the great plains of Altman's precious wide screen, America bustled, hustled and tussled … Who could stop these creatures, or shut them up? Not Altman: he hears America talking, endlessly, engagingly, whether or not it makes sense."

Receiving a Lifetime Achievement Oscar in the spring of 2006, Altman compared the movie process to "making a sand castle at the beach." Actually, his movies were more circuses than castles, and Altman was the ringmaster, using his whip not on the actors (who delighted in the improvisatory freedom he allowed them) but on the audience (whom he wanted to get his point about the erratic, intransigent nature of the modern American). He also revealed in his remarks that he'd had a heart transplant a decade ago. That borrowed heart didn't fail him any more than his corrosive wit did in a 60-year career.

Gordon Parks: American Documentarian

HE WAS THE MAN BEHIND THE LENS, NOT IN FRONT OF IT. In one of his several volumes of published memoirs, Gordon Parks once wrote, "I still don't know exactly who I am. I've disappeared into myself so many different ways that I don't know who 'me' is." Maybe not, although for decades Parks was a very visible artist and trailblazer. But as TIME critic Richard Lacayo noted, the part about "many different ways" certainly rang true. In his 93 years, Parks triumphed in a host of fields—as master photographer; as a writer of novels and memoirs; and as a film director.

The novelist who wrote *The Learning Tree* (and directed the 1969 film version) was also the composer of film scores and concertos; the poet was also the man who directed *Shaft* in 1971 and kicked off Hollywood's blaxploitation era.

The youngest of 15 children in a poor Kansas tenant farm family, Parks scrambled early on, working as a semi-pro basketball player and playing piano in a brothel. He was toiling as a railway waiter in 1938 when he picked up a copy of LIFE and took his first look at the photographs of Depression-era America made by Dorothea Lange and other Farm Security Administration (FSA) photographers. Parks bought a camera and within a few years had become an FSA photographer himself.

On his first day in Washington, Parks was refused service at a clothing store, a movie theater and a restaurant because he was black. But he struggled against social shackles. *The Learning Tree* was the first Hollywood movie written, directed and scored by an African American. Not bad for a man who, Lacayo argued, will be primarily remembered for his classic, indelible photographs. ∎

GORDON PARKS—TIME LIFE PICTURES

The master of all trades in 1948

1950-2006

Wendy Wasserstein: Voice of a Generation—and a Gender

AS SHE LIKED TO TELL THE STORY, WENDY WASSERSTEIN, who grew up in New York City, was inspired to become a playwright by attending Broadway plays and wondering "Where are the girls?" The girls, it turned out, were in her head, and she brought them onstage in a series of well-made plays that portrayed, with acute observation, ironic wit and gentle pathos, the plight of women of her generation. Her breakthrough play, 1977's *Uncommon Women and Others*, which starred Glenn Close, Jill Eikenberry and Swoosie Kurtz, was followed by other hits, including *The Heidi Chronicles* (1989) and *The Sisters Rosensweig* (1993).

Wasserstein's outsize personality and nurturing spirit made her a compelling character in her own right. Eager to experience motherhood, she underwent eight years of fertility treatments that led to the birth of a daughter in 1999, when she was 48. The year before, she launched a program

designed to bring underprivileged students from New York City's public high schools to the theater.

Wasserstein's female characters often seemed trapped between the great expectations fueled by the liberating visions of the feminist movement and the realities of life's limitations—the gradual realization that none of us can, despite society's cheap nostrums, have it all. "The women's movement, the movement that said, 'Your voice is worthwhile,' is the only reason I feel like a person," Wasserstein told PEOPLE magazine in 1990. "But what still needs to change is that women shouldn't beat themselves up for their choices—for being a mother or a single mother, or being a playwright, or being beautiful or not being beautiful. It's important that there isn't one ... slot." Wasserstein, one of the liveliest figures of the American stage, succumbed to complications of lymphoma at 55.

BETTMANN CORBIS

1924-2006
Don Knotts

Television's exposed nerve found early fame playing "Mr. Morrison," the anxious man-in-the-street on Steve Allen's *Tonight Show* in the 1950s. Gulping, perspiring and protesting that he was perfectly at ease, Knotts grew that sketch into a career. When his friend Andy Griffith mentioned that he was going to play a country sheriff in a new sitcom, Knotts suggested he would need a sidekick: thus was born one of TV's most beloved characters, the bumbling, bug-eyed deputy of the mythical small town of Mayberry. Later, as the pseudo-suave Mr. Furley on *Three's Company*, Knotts added leering, laughable libido to his repertoire.

1912-2006
Byron Nelson

The gentlemanly legend of golf had the greatest season in the sport's history in 1945, winning 18 titles, including a still unmatched record of 11 straight tournament victories. The son of Texas cotton farmers, Nelson learned the game after becoming a caddie to earn pocket money. In 1937 he won the Masters and gained the confidence "that I could make good decisions in difficult circumstances." That confidence—and a swing so pure, it's still seen as the paragon—carried him to four more major titles and his historic streak. Nelson's wife had urged him to turn pro as a way of earning enough money to buy the ranch of their dreams. Upon reaching that goal (in 1946), the man other players called Lord Byron retired. "I had a goal," Nelson explained years later. "I could see the prize money going into the ranch, buying a tractor or a cow. It gave me an incentive." Afterward, others' careers became his priority. A natural teacher, he mentored players like Hall of Famer Tom Watson, encouraged a young Tiger Woods and was known for sending pros handwritten letters full of cheer. "I have tried hard to do proper," Nelson said in 2002. "I think I've done a pretty good job."

AP/WIDE WORLD

1921-2006
Lloyd Bentsen

The courtly, influential Senator from Texas and Democratic candidate for Vice President in 1988 was a decorated war hero who was shot down twice over Europe during World War II. As chairman of the Senate Finance Committee from 1987 to 1992 and Bill Clinton's first Treasury Secretary, the pro-business Democrat was widely admired as a bipartisan coalition builder. Clinton declared in eulogizing Bentsen, "[He was] one of the very few candidates for the vice presidency in the history of the Republic who lost and came out better than he went in." He will be remembered for the potent barb he threw when a young Dan Quayle compared himself to John F. Kennedy in a 1988 vice-presidential debate. "Senator," Bentsen said, "I served with Jack Kennedy. I knew Jack Kennedy. Jack Kennedy was a friend of mine. Senator, you're no Jack Kennedy."

DIANA WALKER—TIME LIFE PICTURES—GETTY IMAGES

BETTMANN CORBIS

1924-2006
Sarah Caldwell

"Once in a while [in opera]," conductor Sarah Caldwell told LIFE magazine in 1965, "when everything is just right, there is a moment of magic. People can live on moments of magic." The imaginative founding director of the now-defunct Opera Company of Boston and the first woman to conduct at the New York City Opera lived on such moments, producing some 100 operas over 30 years, including complex modern works like Prokofiev's *War and Peace*. Although her insistence on both directing and conducting could slow production, she was hailed as an inventive artist and a nurturer of emerging singers. A driven eccentric, she often worked around the clock and sometimes slept in theaters where she was staging productions. In 1975 a TIME cover story hailed "Music's Wonder Woman" as the "the best opera director in the U.S."

1934-2006
R.W. Apple Jr.

What a life! Apple was a foreign correspondent who filed dispatches from more than 100 countries; a consummate insider who knew where the bodies were buried from Vietnam to Washington; a gourmet fueled by a legendary expense account. Writing in TIME, his friend Senator John McCain recalled "Johnny" as a Saigon war correspondent:

"He was among the most colorful—generous, imperious, obstinate, quick-witted, contentious and great company." The storied gourmand, whose books on food and wine were highly regarded, possessed what friends called "the best mind and worst body" in American journalism.

1917-2006
Caspar Weinberger

The wry, intellectual public servant's long record of toil in the White Houses of Presidents Nixon, Ford and Reagan was marred by a late blemish: a 1992 indictment for allegedly covering up facts in the Iran-*contra* scandal. He vigorously denied the charges and was later pardoned. As Defense Secretary under Reagan, he presided over a $2 trillion military buildup and backed Reagan's "Star Wars" initiative. After disagreeing with Reagan over arms-control negotiations with the U.S.S.R., he retired in 1987. "I did not arm to attack," he said of his cold war efforts, but "to make war less likely."

1935-2006
Floyd Patterson

The undersized high school dropout from Brooklyn won Olympic gold in 1952. Four years later, at age 21, Floyd Patterson knocked out Archie Moore and become the world's youngest heavyweight champ—as well as its most conflicted. The Hall of Famer, who said he had "no self-esteem" as a kid, was so stung by a 1959 loss to Ingemar Johansson that he left the arena in disguise. Yet when he regained the title from Johansson a year later, he was disturbed by his "hate" for his rival. After retiring, boxing's gentle legend became an ecumenical minister. His last fight, against Alzheimer's and prostate cancer, endured for years. We give it to him on points.

ADRIAN BOOT—RETNA LTD.

ED CLARK—TIME LIFE PICTURES

1914-2006
James Van Allen

In an effort to add a veneer of science to the space race, in 1958 government officials asked James Van Allen to design an experiment for the first U.S. satellite, Explorer 1. He suggested adding a geiger counter, which could detect charged particles— and thus discovered the two doughnut-shaped belts of radioactivity that surround Earth and were later named for him. He was one of 15 scientists named Men of the Year by TIME in 1961. Finding the belts, he later said, "was like going hunting for rabbits and encountering an elephant instead."

1946-2006
Robert (Syd) Barrett

A brilliant, troubled recluse, the original leader of the seminal psychedelic rock band Pink Floyd wrote almost all the group's early music. In 1968, a year after the release of Pink Floyd's acclaimed debut album, *The Piper at the Gates of Dawn*, Barrett left the band following a mental breakdown that was aided, in part, by heavy LSD use. An icon to musicians from David Bowie to Robyn Hitchcock, Barrett lived in obscurity at his mother's house in Cambridge from 1970 until his death. He was saluted by his former bandmates in the songs *Wish You Were Here* and *Shine On You Crazy Diamond*.

AP/WIDE WORLD

CHARLES BONNAY—TIME LIFE PICTURES

1933-2006
Lou Rawls

The singer got his start performing doo-wop with high school pal Sam Cooke before recording soulful tunes in genres from jazz to gospel. Making more than 50 albums over 40 years, the man who Frank Sinatra said had the "silkiest chops in the singing game" topped the R&B charts and crafted pre-rap monologues (*Tobacco Road*). His signature tune was the 1976 megahit *You'll Never Find (Another Love Like Mine)*.

1913-2006
Oleg Cassini

After dressing Marilyn Monroe, onetime fiancé Grace Kelly and second wife Gene Tierney in Hollywood, the pioneer celebrity designer set up shop in New York City in the 1950s, launching still-popular trends like A-line dresses before advising new First Lady Jacqueline Kennedy:"forget about representing the look of the moment, you should have your own look." He soon convinced her that she needed one chief couturier: himself. The Paris-born designer went on to create the elegant ensembles that made Jackie the most stylish, most copied First Lady in U.S. history. Cassini lived, he claimed, by a personal motto: "Be mobile at all times."

RICH PILLING—MLB PHOTOS VIA GETTY IMAGES

1918-2006
Mickey Spillane

The scribe behind the hard-boiled Mike Hammer detective novels appalled critics with his stilted prose. "Her eyes were a symphony of incredulity," Spillane wrote of a "dame" whom Hammer had romanced, then shot. But readers bought more than 100 million Spillane novels, lured by the anti-commie stance and good-vs.-evil plots of such yarns as *My Gun Is Quick; One Lonely Night;* and *I, the Jury.* The hard-drinking, gleefully sadistic Hammer inspired film noir (*Kiss Me, Deadly*), made-for-TV movies and three TV series. Spillane bore similarities to his cavalier hero. "I don't give a hoot about … reviews. What I want to read are royalty checks," he boasted. But he had a subtler side, writing two well-received children's books and parodying his macho image in TV beer ads.

1960-2006
Kirby Puckett

"Tonight I'm drivin' the bus, boys," the Hall of Fame outfielder famously told his Minnesota Twins teammates before Game Six of the 1991 World Series. He proceeded to hit two homers, including a winning 11th-inning dinger that forced a Game Seven, which the Twins won. The Chicago native played his entire career with the Twins, leading them to another World Series victory in 1994 and becoming Minnesota's most revered adopted son. A short, rotund man who seemed to excel through sheer love of the game, Puckett was forced to retire at age 35 due to glaucoma. The 10-time All-Star endured troubled times after his career ended, including multiple brushes with the law. Yet after he died of a sudden, massive stroke, fans and teammates could remember only the glory: the Twins wore his No. 34 on their sleeves throughout the 2006 season.

ART RICKERBY—TIME LIFE PICTURES

IAN SHOWELL—KEYSTONE—GETTY IMAGES

1946-2006
Billy Preston

At age 7, Preston started directing choir sessions at his Los Angeles church; 20 years later, he was rousing far larger audiences with such hits as *Nothing from Nothing* and *Will It Go Round in Circles?* To such musical peers as Bob Dylan and the Beatles, the gregarious, gospel-influenced keyboard virtuoso was the most coveted session player of his era. Preston, said George Harrison, helped keep the Beatles together during their tumultuous late-career *Let It Be* sessions; he famously accompanied them in their last concert, on a London rooftop in 1969. The effervescent artist also wrote the popular standard *You Are So Beautiful* for Joe Cocker. In his later years, the leading R&B piano man of the '60s and '70s was derailed by struggles with alcohol abuse and cocaine addiction.

June Allyson

June Allyson, 88, wholesome, gravel-voiced Hollywood star and epitome of the "girl next door" for her frequent turns in the '40s and '50s as a loyal, adoring girlfriend or wife.

Arnold (Red) Auerbach, 89, cigar-chomping Hall of Fame coach of the Boston Celtics and creator of one of the great franchises in sports history; he drafted Larry Bird and coached the likes of Bill Russell and Bob Cousy to nine NBA championships.

Peter Benchley, 65, author who made landlubbers of millions with his 1974 novel *Jaws,* about a great white shark that terrorizes an otherwise idyllic East Coast resort town.

P.W. Botha, 90, an unapologetic advocate of apartheid and South Africa's leader from 1978-89. He met secretly with the jailed Nelson Mandela and saw the country's policy of strict racial segregation begin to unravel within months of his resignation.

Red Buttons, 87, impish and widely loved funnyman who emerged from burlesque to forge an acclaimed acting career spanning more than 30 films, including *They Shoot Horses, Don't They?* and *The Poseidon Adventure.*

Otis Chandler, 78, visionary publisher of the family-owned Los Angeles *Times* during the 1960s and '70s. He transformed it into one of the country's finest dailies.

Betty Comden, 89, sophisticated, witty wordsmith who, with her collaborator of 60 years, Adolph Green, helped create stage musicals like *On the Town* and *Bells Are Ringing* and wrote screenplays for the films *Singin' in the Rain* and *The Band Wagon.*

Mike Douglas, 81, ever polite, even-keeled—and hugely successful—early TV talk-show host whose 90-min. gabfest aired from 1961 to 1982.

Katherine Dunham, 96, anthropologist and choreographer who founded the first black modern-dance company in the U.S. and influenced artists from Alvin Ailey to James Dean with her Dunham Technique, a blend of Afro-Caribbean folk, classical and modern movement.

Barbara Epstein, 77, literary lion who as a founder and co-editor of the *New York Review of Books* worked with and befriended such writers as Joyce Carol Oates, Desmond Tutu, Vaclav Havel and Alison Lurie.

Freddy Fender, 69, a three-time Grammy winner who took his stage name from his favorite brand of guitar but began his career as "El Bebop Kid," singing Elvis songs in Spanish. In 1975 he topped the pop and country charts with *Before the Next Teardrop Falls.*

Glenn Ford, 90, nice-guy leading man who won consistent critical praise over a career that spanned a half-century and more than 80 films. Wearing the white hat in westerns,

Red Buttons

comedies and thrillers, including *The Blackboard Jungle* and *Pocketful of Miracles,* Ford epitomized decency and strength.

Pierre Gemayel, 34, Lebanon's outspoken Minister of Industry and son of former President Amin Gemayel who was shot by three gunmen at point-blank range in Beirut. He was Lebanon's fifth anti-Syrian leader to be assassinated in the past two years.

Curt Gowdy, 86, longtime "voice of the Boston Red Sox" and NBC sports broadcasts who was as beloved by fans as by the athletes whose exploits he narrated in memorable fashion.

Jane Jacobs, 89, self-taught guru of urban planning whose clear, sensible voice appealing for a neighborhood approach to big-city living—most famously in her seminal 1961 book, *The Death and Life of Great American Cities*—revolutionized the field.

Bruno Kirby, 57, high-pitched, piquant actor and cult favorite who infused his many supporting roles—often as best friend or oddball—with subtle intensity and wry humor. His 35-year career spanned *The Godfather, Good Morning Vietnam* and *When Harry Met Sally* ...

Jeane Kirkpatrick, 80, Ronald Reagan's first ambassador to the United Nations; she abandoned the Democratic Party to become a leading voice of neoconservative Republicanism.

Patricia Kennedy Lawford, 82, sister of President John F. Kennedy who married British-born actor and playboy Peter Lawford; they divorced in 1966. A socialite and world traveler, she was considered the most sophisticated of the renowned Kennedy siblings.

Gyorgy Ligeti, 83, Hungarian avant-garde composer who, in spite of his staunch refusal to seek popular acceptance, gained global fame when, to his surprise, Stanley Kubrick used his eerie music in the 1968 film *2001: A Space Odyssey.*

Arnold Newman, 88, who snapped 49¢

Maureen Stapleton

portraits before creating the classic photographs that graced the covers of LIFE, *Look* and other publications. In Newman's technique, "environmental portraiture," subjects are seen immersed in objects that telegraph the essence of their works.

Fayard Nicholas, 91, tap dancer extraordinaire who, performing with brother Harold as the Nicholas Brothers, performed gravity-defying fantasias with his feet, inspiring generations of airborne dancers from Fred Astaire to Savion Glover.

Buck Owens, 76, singer of more than 20 No. 1 country hits and longtime co-host of the hayseed variety show *Hee Haw,* he pioneered country music's raw, roadhousey "Bakersfield sound."

Wilson Pickett, 64, volatile R&B star (and Rock and Roll Hall of Famer) whose gravelly, raunchy delivery on such 1960s hits as the cowbell-driven *Mustang Sally* and saucy *In the Midnight Hour* helped earn him the moniker Wicked Pickett.

Augusto Pinochet, 91, the general who became dictator of Chile after helping lead a coup that toppled the democratically elected leftist Salvador Allende in 1973. Thousands of political opponents were killed or "disappeared" under the brutal regime of Pinochet, yet although he was briefly arrested and held while visiting Britain for medical treatment in 1998, he was released because of his advanced age and poor health, and he never stood trial for the abuses that occurred during his 17 years in power.

John Profumo, 91, former British War Minister who resigned from the Cabinet in 1963 after lying to Parliament about his affair with a prostitute, Christine Keeler, then 19, whose other clients included a Soviet diplomat.

A.M. Rosenthal, 84, venerated, loathed, combative editor credited with reviving the New York *Times* during the financially strapped 1970s and transforming the Gray Lady into a fat, engaging, reader-friendly daily.

Joe Rosenthal, 94, Associated Press combat photographer who in 1945 captured the iconic image of U.S. troops raising the Stars and Stripes atop Mount Suribachi on Iwo Jima. After missing an earlier flag raising, the diminutive photojournalist heard that a grander flag was being hoisted. Clambering onto a pile of rocks to get his angle, he snapped just in time. Later, mortified by the hoopla over the image, he said, "I took it, but the Marines took Iwo Jima."

Moira Shearer, 80, exquisite, flame-haired prima ballerina whose brief,

Shelley Winters

stellar career as a principal dancer with Britain's famed Sadler's Wells Ballet was overshadowed, to her dismay, by her lead role in the 1948 ballet film *The Red Shoes.*

Norman Shumway, 83, who became in 1968 the first physician to perform a successful heart transplant in the U.S.; he later found ways to dramatically improve the survival rate of transplant recipients.

Muriel Spark, 88, British author of poetry, short stories and more than 20 novels. Her elegantly spare, often-satirical writing (such as her best-known novel, 1961's *The Prime of Miss Jean Brodie*) explored morality and perceptions of truth.

Aaron Spelling, 83, gentle, trailblazing (and prolific) TV tycoon who transformed prime time with series like *Beverly Hills 90210, Melrose Place, Charlie's Angels, The Love Boat, Fantasy Island, Hart to Hart, Twin Peaks* and *The Mod Squad,* among others.

Maureen Stapleton, 80, brilliant, defiantly unglamorous actress who, despite an utterly unpretentious style — "the main thing is to keep the audience awake," she said of her craft—won awards and critical raves for astute, rich performances over her 60-year career.

Jack Warden, 85, prizefighter turned tough guy of stage and screen who appeared in nearly 100 films over five decades, including *12 Angry Men, All the President's Men* and *The Verdict.*

Dennis Weaver, 81, gangly cowpoke actor best known as the limping sidekick in *Gunsmoke* and as the titular, Manhattan cowboy cop in the 1970s series *McCloud.*

Shelley Winters, 85, zaftig, high-decibel star and two-time Oscar winner who played some of the movies' most famous victims. She was strangled by Ronald Colman (*A Double Life*), drowned by Montgomery Clift (*A Place in the Sun*) and had her throat slit by Robert Mitchum (*The Night of the Hunter*).